A GAME OF SOLDIERS

To Alice & Alan
from
Hugh

with every best wish!

A GAME OF SOLDIERS
1957–60

By

Hugh T. Grant

BEAULIEU BOOKS

Published and distributed by
Beaulieu Books
94a Old Edinburgh Road,
Inverness
IV2 3HT
Tel: (01463) 222349   Fax: (01463 715868)
E-mail   grant@heraldry.co.uk

First published 2001

ISBN 0-9539810-0-2

Prepared for publication by Jim Thomson Graphic Design
Forbes House, Great North Road, Muir of Ord IV6 7TP

Printed and bound in Great Britain
by Butler & Tanner Ltd., Frome and London.

CONTENTS

FOREWORD

By John Ridgway MBE

Draining the heart of Loch Ness, the river runs through the centre of Inverness, in grey January it is a vein of liquid ice. Well muffled up, I bumped into Hugh Grant on the street, each of us eager to be on his way. He mentioned he was writing a book about his National Service in the Parachute Regiment.

"What's your number?" I muttered. "23525694!" he chuckled.

"I'm 23341259!" says I "What's the title?"

"A Game of Soldiers".

"That's just what I think about this weather – I'm off!"

Hurrying on my way, I marvelled at how I could remember those eight digits, at the drop of a hat, after nearly half a century. I couldn't tell you my car number. But the title ";*:# that for a game of soldiers!" has seldom been far from my lips. I ran away to sea at seventeen, to be a cadet in the Clan Line, aboard a cargo ship. I chipped rust off that wartime relic all the way out to Portuguese East Africa. But eight knots was too slow, the shared cabin too cramped and I walked away when we got back to Salford Docks in Manchester.

"You've made a mess of choosing a career, now you'll go into insurance!" snorted my Father. National Service was inevitable; there was nothing voluntary about it. I rushed out and had my call up accelerated, never thinking of all the other young men being drawn to the same experience, at the same time.

A few weeks later, just eighteen, I was in Malvern, training to become a Sapper, because my father was a civil engineer. Eric Stonehouse was a gentle giant from Newcastle, and a welder by trade. Sitting on my bed in the barrack-room one November evening, I was bulling my boots. Eric was pressing a pair of battledress trousers with the squad steam iron, using brown paper as an additional shield against the heat. His bed was three up from mine, and on the other side of the hut. We were all working away at our kit, we all hated the Corporal, we all hated the Army – it wasn't very difficult to hate each other. With my back turned to Eric, I was concentrating hard, the shine had to be immaculate. I was unaware of the rising tempers, as the usual banter became more and more personal. Everyone teased Eric about his broad Geordie accent; without thinking I joined in.

"Look out, Ridge!" someone shouted.

I leapt to my feet and as I turned Eric grabbed the lapels of my battledress and heaved me towards him, smashing his forehead down on my nose as he did so. Luckily he didn't follow this up with the customary knee in the groin.

Our room mates dragged us apart as the blood streamed down my face. I protested in vain that we should go out into the dark and settle it; he could have killed me.

Eric had 'stuck the nut' on me. I have never forgotten the lesson. An aggressor with the benefit of surprise, should cripple his opponent with the first series of blows. Subsequently, I have enjoyed success with a counter to this particular and widely used ganbit: this is to drop the chin on the chest and slightly anticipate the butt. This results in the aggressor butting his face on the hard dome of the victim's head with the combined weight of both bodies and the neck muscles of the aggressor. The victim, thus gaining the initiative, should follow up with the knee to the groin. To the alert, a second can seem as long as an hour.

After a couple if years at R.M.A. Sandhurst, in line with a change of policy, I was commissioned directly into the Parachute Regiment. As Hugh mentions, Rudge Penley was the first, he was posted to 1 PARA; Pat Wood and I followed, to 2 and 3 PARA respectively. But first I had to pass 'P' Company. There were desperate men. I'll never forget that 'P' Course. The Milling and being tricked into a second fight with the biggest fellow on the course. Losing my grip and belly-flopping off the trapeze over the swimming pool. Collapsing at the end of the Log Race and finding the toggle rope cut deep into my hand and I'd never even felt it. The reward was the fierce sense of achievement and the comradeship. Regimental Pride and intense loyalty seem far distant nowadays.

But I do remember the simple brutality of it all. It was hardly the 'Nanny State'. It marked us all and not all of the two million or so young men who underwent National Service between 1947 and 1960 were suited to the experience. And unfortunately it was the more delicate flowers, the small minority who just could not adapt, who found themselves spending long months in holding companies or in 'tin rooms' scrubbing greasy pans: for them, perhaps it really was two years wasted.

Hugh's humorous narrative illustrates the positive side. For all those who 'did their National Service' it is a vivid reminder of good times and bad, a very personal time of real living. Those unlucky enough to miss the experience can read this book and join the great debate: would two years of discipline for 18–20 year olds help this nation today?

John Ridgway MBE
School of Adventure,
Rhiconich, By Lairg, Sutherland IV27 4RB
November 2000.

Footnote – John Ridgway, while still a serving officer in the Parachute Regiment, celebrated 1966 by rowing across the Atlantic with Chay Blyth. Both were awarded the MBE in 1967. In 1969 John and his wife Marie Christine founded their renowned School of Adventure at Ardmore on Scotland's rugged west coast. Along with running the school John has gone on to forge a considerable international reputation as a sailor, explorer and author. Even now he is planning a non-stop solo circumnavigation of the World in August 2003 to mark his becoming a senior citizen!

ACKNOWLEDGMENTS

So there it is! A long forgotten sort of diary that I kept intermittently during my National Service days is at last a book. Much of the blame for this can be laid directly at the doors of John Cairney and Iain R. Thomson who goaded and prompted me into action. Special thanks to John and Alannah in distant New Zealand for a long and highly valued friendship. Thanks also to Iain for advice and encouragement at a critical stage. Why did I write the book? Many reasons but for so many years when I spoke to fellow National Servicemen the most common refrain was that it was at best a waste of time. I know that distance lends enchantment but for me my days in the Paras were 'the golden years'! It was exciting times and I was young, healthy, foot loose and fiancée free with little or no responsibility on my shoulders.

My military service also gave me the privilege of forming deep and lasting friendships with a colourful array of characters that endure to this day.

In no special order I list as follows:

George and June Brown – George who on learning that I was to write a book about my army experiences, speaking with all the authority of 32 years service behind him, and in his usual forthright manner declared "What! You write a book – you weren't in the Army for five bloody minutes!"

To Paddy and Maree Tomkins: Arthur and Brenda Liles; Jim and Hazel Hunt: Frank and Helen Brady: Henry and Margaret Armstrong: Jim and Nancy Wilkie: David 'Mitch' Mitchell.

So many others who passed like ships in the night.

Grateful acknowledgments go to–

John Ridgway for doing the foreword to my book and for his bold, buccaneering outlook on life that for me epitomises all that is best in the Paras.

Andy Lee – deputy News Editor of the South Shields Gazette.

Trish Smart of Jim Thomson Graphic Design for her highly imaginative treatment of the book's front cover.

Mrs Brinton – Past Editor of the Pegasus Magazine.

To all my fellow members of the Highlands and Islands Branch of the Parachute Regimental Association for their interest and support.

Elder brother Gerry who went before me into N.S. and pointed the way.

To youngest son Jonathan for his efforts in distributing the book.

Last but not least – to my beautiful wife Joan who always believed in me even during the dark days and has been my soul mate and anchor in what has been a reasonably turbulent life.

Hugh T. Grant
Inverness – December 2000

"A Game of Soldiers 1957–60" is dedicated to:

All those who wore the red beret since the formation of Airborne Forces –
in particular all those who gave their lives in service and for whom surely
the trumpets have sounded on the other side.

EXPLANATION OF BOOK TITLE

We paraded after lunch in front of the Recruit Company billet. Some forty-eight ill-assorted individuals–all hopeful to join the ranks of the elite Parachute Regiment. Many of us were still in our civilian clothes whereas others were trying to look the part in ill-fitting denims and shirts, newly issued from the Quartermaster's stores.

The Corporal in charge walked us through the lines to a recreational hall. Inside, chairs were arranged in rows facing a cinema screen. We filed in and took our seats. After a considerable delay, an officer appeared and explained to us that we were about to be shown a unique film. Entitled "For Theirs was the Glory", it had been filmed in 1945 in Arnhem just after World War 2 had finished. It depicted the events of September 1944 when the 1st Airborne Division had landed at Arnhem in an ill-fated attempt to seize and hold the bridge across the Neder Rhine.

Apparently, showing this film was part of our induction process. The lights in the hall were put out. The film projector clattered into action and the opening titles flashed up on the screen. For the next hour, we sat enthralled as this remarkable piece of cinematic history unfolded. The action was very realistic and the room fairly reverberated to the crackle of small arms fire, the crump of mortars and the blast of tank fire. Eventually, the film came to an end, the end titles came up on the screen and the projector fell silent. The lights were switched on and a strange silence settled on the room as we reflected on what we had seen. Bob Ward chose this moment to pass an aside to the person sitting next to him. Unfortunately, it was only too audible as it broke the silence. "F#*k that for a game of soldiers!"

CHAPTER 1

BACKGROUND TO NATIONAL SERVICE

National Service was borne out of the carnage that was the First World War. Lord Kitchener, at the outset of the war in 1914, was convinced that compulsory National Service was not necessary to raise men for the Army. Alfred Leete's famous poster of Lord Kitchener as a messianic recruiting officer with his pointed command "YOUR COUNTRY NEEDS YOU" would suffice. However, in 1915, voluntary recruitment had slumped, as the first heady days of a rush to the Colours had passed. Even Phyllis Done's famous call to arms in the popular music hall song "We don't want to lose you, but we think you ought to go" was falling on deaf ears.

In 1916, the National Service Bill was passed requiring all males over 18 years of age to report for military service.

In 1939, at the outset of World War 2, Prime Minister Chamberlain explained in a radio broadcast:

"Compulsion is not in accordance with the democratic system under which we live, or consistent with the tradition of freedom which we have always striven to maintain. We are confident that we shall get all the volunteers we want without recourse to compulsion."

In March 1947, another National Service Bill was passed. Such was the opposition that the period was reduced from 18 months to 12 months. Within a year it had been extended to 18 months and in 1950 two years. Some two million conscripts underwent National Service from 1945 to 1963 when such service was finally abolished.

These conscripts abandoned their civilian lives to serve as soldiers, sailors and airmen in the Colours of the Monarch.

Too young to vote, but old enough to kill or be killed, these legions of fresh faced eighteen year olds were to garrison in Germany in the lowered temperatures of the Cold War and oversee the dismantling of an empire. They served at home and abroad–in Europe, the Middle and Far East. Many saw action in Korea, Malaya and Cyprus.

1

The forces gained most from National Service as they were provided with a large and regular intake of well nourished and well educated young men with a variety of skills.

Young men were plunged, at an impressionable age, into the hurly burly of Service life and had to adapt to it as best they could.

For most, it was a rough sort of "finishing school" in which they would mix and live with a cross section of their fellow countrymen, visit places that otherwise they would never have seen and face a variety of new experiences.

As we enter a new century it is now almost forty years since the Forces said farewell to the last National Serviceman. An entire generation has emerged who never had to answer the call to Service life and National Service itself has been relegated to a mere footnote in British Military History.

CHAPTER 2

THE JOURNEY TO ALDERSHOT

"O, why the deuce should I repine,
And be an ill foreboder?
I'm twenty three and five feet nine,
I'll go and be a sodger!"
                                    Robert Burns

The train journey from Waterloo Station to Aldershot takes about an hour. It gave me plenty of time, that sultry afternoon of Thursday 11th July 1957 to reflect on my life up until this point–all nineteen years of it.

I glanced again at the letter in my hand. It instructed me in formal military style to report on this date to Maida Barracks in Aldershot, home of the Recruit Company of the Parachute Regiment.

Furthermore, I was to make myself available between 1400 hours and 1700 hours. I tucked the letter away carefully in my jacket pocket, leaned back and stretched my legs. The train, now clear of the station, began to sway and pick up speed as it headed towards Aldershot.

****

For me, life had run along pretty conventional lines up until this point. My family home was a croft or small holding some ten miles due North of Inverness, self-styled capital of the Highlands. I was the second oldest in a family of four boys and one girl. Most crofters, despite working their own small crofts, required to have another job to support their families. In this my father was no exception, and worked as a collection agent for the Refuge Assurance Company, that involved him cycling round a large scattered rural area.

The village of Beauly, some three miles away, was where my parents had first set up house when they married in 1935. It was there that I was born in September 1937. Beauly has a long history with evidence that the area had been inhabited for over 4000 years. This is supported by the fact

3

that remains of crannogs, or man made islands built as forts in times of danger, have been found in the Firth. In the surrounding hills, signs of vitrified forts underline this early occupation.

The main features are a large village square and the ruins of a 13th Century Priory. Beauly is said to have got its name from the ill-fated Mary Queen of Scots who visited the village in 1574. She is said to have described it as "beau lieu" or 'beautiful place.'

This is Clan Fraser territory with Beaufort Castle the seat of the Frasers of Lovat a few miles away. Not surprisingly, we lived in Fraser Street!

The military came to play quite a prominent part in my early life. This might come as a surprise because in no way was Beauly recognised as a garrison town and my family most certainly had no military connection.

The reason was that exactly one week short of my second birthday, the Second World War broke out on Sunday 3rd September 1939.

My childhood recollections of wartime Beauly are understandably somewhat disjointed. The first clear memory that I have is of being held in my mother's arms at a window as a multi-coloured stream of horses stampeded down the narrow confines of Fraser Street and of women screaming. A detachment of Lovat Scouts had been based at Muir of Ord a couple of miles away over the Ross-shire border. One morning in November 1939, for some reason, the horses broke loose and galloped down the road to Beauly, where eventually they were rounded up. As things went, it was a very exciting event for the village and certainly for an infant just over two years old! My childhood companion was my elder brother, Gerry, and Fraser Street was our patch. As war time rationing took effect, our mother had made us both a pair of red dungarees out of some scrap material, so we cut a fairly distinctive figure as we moved about our fiefdom.

From an early age, I loved to wander and this caused my mother some considerable concern. At one end of the village, stood the Lovat Arms Hotel where a barrier had been erected complete with two sentry boxes. All traffic heading North was stopped by the sentries, passes checked and then the barrier raised in order to allow the vehicle to pass. There was much saluting and stamping of feet which added greatly to the spectacle. For some reason, I found this utterly fascinating and would stand for ages gravely watching the whole process.

The other focal point of my attention was the Boer War Monument to the Lovat Scouts that dominated the village square. This towering stone edifice had been erected in 1905 when the Scouts had returned from the South African Campaign. Three of the four sided monument bore the names of the places where the Scouts had seen action–

DIAMOND HILL–CAPE COLONY–WITTEBERGEN. There were also panels engraved with the names of those who had fallen in action or died of disease.

At the outbreak of the Boer War, the British military authorities were found wanting. Soldiers in bright red uniforms trained for 19th Century warfare were ill-equipped to deal with the dogged guerrilla tactics adopted by the highly mobile, mounted Boer farmers. As a result, the war dragged on and became something of an embarrassment. Lord Lovat, the local Clan Chief, realising that the Boers had to be fought on their own terms raised a regiment of Lovat Scouts. These men were drawn from his own clansmen and estate workers. Men naturally trained in fieldcraft, spying and reconnaissance as well as being crackshots with the rifle. In short, they were a hardy and valiant breed and ideal for pitting against the Boers and went on to distinguish themselves in the South African campaign.

The main inscription on the monument read:

ERECTED
BY THE LOVAT TENANTRY AND FEUARS
OF THE AIRD AND FORT AUGUSTUS DISTRICT
TO COMMEMORATE
THE RAISING OF THE LOVAT SCOUTS
FOR SERVICE IN SOUTH AFRICA
BY SIMON JOSEPH 16th LORD LOVAT
CVO–CB–DSO
WHO DESIRED TO SHEW
THAT THE MARTIAL SPIRIT OF THEIR FOREFATHERS
STILL ANIMATES
THE HIGHLANDERS OF TODAY
AND WHOSE CONFIDENCE WAS JUSTIFIED
BY THEIR SUCCESS IN THE FIELD
OF GALLANT CORPS
WHOSE EXISTENCE WAS DUE
TO HIS LOYALTY AND PATRIOTISM
AD 1905

Not that at my tender age was I really able to understand the writing on the monument panels. What did attract me was a raised three dimensional feature on the side that faced the main road. It depicted two Lovat Scouts wearing their distinctive slouch hats. One figure was holding the reins of a horse pawing the ground with one hoof and neck arched. The other Scout was squatting with a field telescope to his eye scanning the hot dusty veldt for signs of enemy movement.

This scene as if frozen in time allowed my imagination to run riot and I yearned for the day when I would grow up and be able to ride a horse wearing a slouch hat.

The Grant family had little or no military tradition despite the fact that two World Wars had taken place in the first half of the 20th century. Somehow we had been posted absent and missed out.

My father, born in 1900, had been called up in September 1918 when he had attained his eighteenth birthday. He reported with others to nearby Fort George and then had to kick his heels as World War 1 ground to a halt. His intake were never issued with uniforms, far less rifles. When peace was finally declared on 11th November 1918, they were sent home post haste as the Army prepared to handle the demobilisation of hundreds of thousands of serving troops. When World War 2 broke out he rushed to the colours only to be told that as a father of a young family, as well as being almost forty years old, that his services were not required.

Like many other men in his position he joined the Home Guard. They would parade in the evenings on a regular basis under the command of Charlie Cameron, the local butcher, who had seen service in the Great War.

Their main function was to patrol at night the high ground above Beauly, known as the Beauly Braes, in the event of an attack by German paratroopers. I have a memory of watching my mother helping to tie the collar on my father's battledress uniform prior to an evening parade.

Even at my tender age I figured that the Beauly Braes did not rank very high among the strategic targets of the German High Command. Still, I suppose it had to be covered, and the local men felt that they were doing their bit.

Down the street from our house, and across the busy A9 road, lay the village Catholic primary school. Immediately behind the school, and close to the ruined Priory, lay a stretch of waste ground. An encampment of black Nissan huts sprung up almost overnight and became the base for a detachment of Polish troops. This, naturally, became a new and exciting area to be explored. We would wander among the huts and soon became quite accepted by the soldiers. I loved looking into the cookhouse with its warm cooking smells, and mounds of peeled potatoes. In one of the huts was a gramophone presented by some local person along with a supply of heavy black records. I suppose it was intended as a welcoming gift to the young Polish soldiers. The gramophone was a bulky instrument with a large horn to amplify the sound and had to be wound up by hand before a record was played. We soon became adept at operating it and would lift the large black record on to the rest and then swing the arm holding the needle carefully on to the record. After some initial scratching sounds the music would burst forth. My favourite record, as I remember, was one entitled, "Don't Sit Under the Apple Tree With Anyone Else But Me!".

One day in the billet as I was doing my disc jockey routine and the soldiers were all lying on their beds smoking and reading, I was in the process of changing a record when suddenly one of the Polish soldiers started to sing: slowly at first and then his voice sounded stronger. It was probably an old Polish folk song, and as he sang the other soldiers fell silent and then one by one they joined in the singing. It was like being caught in the middle of a male voice choir and the Nissan hut fairly rang to the sound. Here they were, these young men in a foreign country singing of home and a home that they did not know if they would ever see again. The sheer intensity and emotion expressed in their singing frightened me. I took to my heels and ran all the way home filled with a nameless dread. It was some time before I could be persuaded to return to the Nissan hut area.

For my first year in school in 1942 I attended the Catholic primary school at the bottom of our street. One day at playtime we came out to find a workman cutting and removing the iron railings from the wall round the school bordering the main road. All over the country such iron work was being removed and sent to munition factories and suchlike as part of the national war effort.

We children gathered round the kneeling workman, with his visor in place, as his acetylene torch bit into the metal bars emitting a shower of sparks. This was really exciting stuff. The workman gradually became aware of his rapt audience of infants. He switched off his torch and raised his visor, "Do you want to know what I am going to do with them?" he asked, gesturing towards the pile of removed metal bars. We all nodded eagerly. "Well, I'm going to take them away and melt them into a huge bomb and then drop it on Mr. Hitler's head!". We were called back to class more than satisfied with the fact that our school was doing its bit.

That evening, back home, my father had to field some urgent questions from me: How did one make a bomb?, How big would it be, and what colour?, Who was this Mr. Hitler?, and lastly, would we get our railings back after the bomb was dropped? I seem to recall being less than satisfied with the answers that I received.

My last real youthful military experience made a real impression on me–and almost a permanent one!

At school lunchtime Gerry and I would cross the main road and run home for our lunch. One day we were returning to school sucking on a slice of orange, when we were joined by two other children. We all stopped

by the busy main road waiting for a break in the traffic, and an
opportunity to cross. I must have been distracted by something or other,
for when I next looked Gerry and the others had crossed the road.
Without any thought, I nipped into the flow of traffic, in order to join
them. There was a loud squeal of brakes, as a large Army truck bore down
on me, and attempted to stop. I had a glimpse of the driver's horrified
expression as he literally stood on his brakes. The truck seemed to rear up
and the bar at the front caught me a glancing blow, sending me flying
under the wheels. The usually noisy playground was silenced and passers-
by stood looking on in shock. I soon broke the spell by emerging from
under the truck bawling my eyes out, and bewailing the loss of my orange
slice. My mother, alerted by the commotion, raced down the street to
claim me, and I was taken home and put to bed to await examination by
the village doctor. In truth I was fine apart from a bruise on my forehead
and a grazed hand. The whole school had to undergo a lecture on the
benefits of road safety and drill by Sergeant Black the local policeman.
That evening the shaken driver and his mate called on me to see how I
was, and brought me a bag of much appreciated sweets.

I quite enjoyed sitting up in bed and being the centre of attraction
because I knew it would not last for long.

It might in fact have all ended there but for my father learning that the
truck driver was to face a military enquiry into a possible dangerous
driving charge. On the day of the Hearing my father put me on the cross
bar of his bike, and cycled up to the military camp at Muir of Ord. I
remember little of the actual enquiry, except for being in a room with lots
of saluting and stamping of feet. My friend the truck driver was standing
in the middle of the room. I waved to him, but strangely enough, he was
looking very serious and did not respond. Suddenly, my father was on his
feet speaking and very shortly the whole thing was over. The older officer,
who seemed to be in charge of things, came over to shake my hand and
look at the fast disappearing bruise on my forehead. We were then taken
to a place called the Mess–but it looked tidy enough to me!–where
everybody had a celebratory drink and I was given a glass of lemonade.
My truck driver friend looked happy, which pleased me, and I was carried
round the room on several khaki clad shoulders. Another glass of
lemonade, and then all too soon it was time to go home.

As we cycled home, I gripped the handlebars of the bike and pretended
I was riding home on horseback from some glorious campaign. Then I
would be able to laugh with others and celebrate our exploits in a place
called the Mess. So, these military seeds were sewn at an early and
impressionable age. However, fate intervened just as the war was hotting

up nicely. My father took ill with a thrombosis, and was laid off work indefinitely. My parents decided to sell up their house in Beauly, and take possession of a small croft cottage that my mother had inherited some twelve miles away in Strathglass. For my parents it was a step back into the dark ages, literally, as the cottage had no electricity, running water or inside toilet. On the other hand for Gerry and I, once we had got over the initial disappointment of leaving wartime Beauly, it was the start of a great new adventure.

We ran wild in the hills round our new residence, and attended the local Struy school, where we soon made new friends. Our water supply was a burn that tumbled down the steep hillside past the cottage. In summer time the water dwindled to a trickle, and we would use the stream as our own personal assault course. The bed of the burn was littered with large boulders, and we would race up stream in bare feet jumping from boulder to boulder. In time a proper water supply was piped in from a hillside spring. The plus side of this move was that wartime rationing hardly impinged upon us as like most country folk our croft and livestock made us virtually self sufficient. Our father, an ex-ghillie, showed us how to fish the River Glass and stalk, taking the occasional red deer from the high hills above the croft.

We still avidly followed the progress of the war. Each day the mail bus that served the glen would pass our cottage, and a rolled up copy of the Daily Express would be thrown out from the speeding vehicle. In the Express we would follow the latter stages of the war as the Allied Forces first stormed ashore in Normandy and then closed in on Berlin. There would be inset maps with arrows showing the approach of the Allies from the west and the Russian army from the east. Sibling rivalry being what it is, Gerry and I took opposing sides–I backed the Allies whereas Gerry took the side of the Red Army in the race to see who would be the first to Berlin. We had a well thumbed school atlas, to help us follow things more closely and see the wider picture. I still claim I would have won the race to the German capital if it had not been for setbacks at Arnhem and the Battle of the Bulge!

And then, all too suddenly the war in Europe was over. Almost overnight, it seemed, we slipped into the Cold War that was destined to dominate our young lives for decades ahead. After seven years in Strathglass, our parents made the decision to move back to Beauly, and into one of the newly built council houses in Aird Road. We found Beauly much changed as men folk returned from the Services, and everybody struggled with post war austerity and continued rationing. The black Nissan huts behind the school were still there, but unoccupied. The Polish soldiers had long since dispersed, save for a few who had courted and married local girls.

We settled down to complete our education in the local school. Gerry left school at fifteen, to become a telegram boy in Inverness. This took the strain off the family purse to some extent, and allowed me to further my academic career.

In my last year in Beauly school, I was one of four pupils following an academic course–my fellow pupils being Finlay MacRae, Tony Macleod and David Fraser. Towards the end of our third and final year, we were obliged to sit a special examination. Passing this examination would mean that we could continue our academic career in the Inverness Royal Academy for a further three years leading to possible university entrance.

The headmaster of the Beauly school, Mr. Eunson, clearly had no high hopes for our quartet because he asked us to give due thought to what jobs we would like to take up when the forthcoming examination found us out. For reasons that now escape me I decided to apply for a position as an artificer apprentice engineer in the Royal Navy. The forms duly arrived, were filled in, and ready to be sent when word came through that we had all passed the examination and gained access to the Inverness Royal Academy. We all accepted, and the course of our lives for the next three years was determined.

In our last year in Beauly, our Geography teacher, Miss Maclean, was exchanged with an American teacher, a Mrs Knox, a widowed lady from Tennessee. She taught Geography in such an interesting way, that I longed to visit the various countries that we studied. Mrs Knox had a certain dress that she wore a lot, and attached to the collar was a pair of leather thongs that hung down to her waist. On the end of these thongs was a brown leather like pouch that contained something that rattled. She explained to us that she had bought it on a trip to an Indian reservation in Arizona, that it was made from buffalo hide, and the pouch held the actual rattle, taken from a rattlesnake! The Indians used to catch the snakes, kill them to remove the rattle and then dry it out in the sun before attaching the buffalo thongs, and then selling the finished article to eager tourists. We accepted this at face value, until Tony MacLeod came up with what he claimed was the correct version. According to Tony it was really the preserved testicles of her late spouse, and the rattler story was just a cover. Mrs Knox had a habit of twirling the leather thongs in her hand as she lectured to us, and could never quite grasp how her pupils found the topography of Scandinavia, a subject of such stifled hilarity.

The three years in the Academy flew past, and I found that I was the only one of our quartet to complete the course. Not I hasten to add, due to any academic brilliance on my part. My parents were keen to see one of their offspring get to university, and I hung on, more out of a sense of duty to them. I had no idea of what I intended to do as a career, and so not really focussed, I drifted, and concentrated more on my sporting life. With a considerable slice of Beauly's eighteen to twenty year olds off doing their National Service, I managed to get a place in the village shinty team. This team, under the able captaincy of "Rox" Maclean, was sweeping all before it as Scottish Junior Champions in the Season 1955–56. At one and the same time, I was playing for the Academy Football XI, who went on that year to win the North of Scotland Schools Cup. On many occasions, I would find myself playing football for the school in the morning, and then rushing to catch the Beauly shinty bus, to turn out for the team in the afternoon.

This pleasant way of life could not continue for ever. At the end of my third and final year, my neglect of any real sustained effort in my studies came home to roost. I ended up just short of enough exam passes to gain entry to university. It was decided that I would re-sit one exam in the autumn in order to put this matter to rights.

I still had no clear idea of what I wanted to do, and this was make your mind up time. In desperation, and coming from a crofting background, I thought that I would do a degree in agriculture. It was then arranged that I would do a year's practical work–six months on a dairy farm and six months on a beef/arable farm.

To this end, I secured an initial six months stint at Erchless Castle Dairy Farm in Strathglass, and would live in lodgings with the MacDonnell family who were caretakers of the village hall.

I commenced work there in June 1956, the day after I left the Academy, and my school days behind.

The Erchless estate was owned by a very colourful character called Baron Stackelberg; a White Russian who had fled his country after the Communist Revolution. He had married into money, and with his wife, had set up home in Erchless Castle, original sea of the Clan Chisholm, and entered into a new life as a Highland estate owner.

The dairy farm boasted of a large herd of Jersey cattle and its milk output was much in demand.

Equally colourful, was the dairy farm manager, one Iain Thomson, who later in life carved out a considerable career as a farmer and author.

I enjoyed enormously working in the open air, and the physical side of the work. Even the daily rising at 5am, I took in my stride. My job, at this unearthly hour, was to round up the herd of cattle from the field where they grazed, and then drive them up the long castle drive, to the dairy where they were to be milked.

One crisp November morning, I rose as usual, and made a quick cup of tea as I prepared for work. An item on the radio caught my attention. Something to the effect that British paratroopers were dropping onto an airfield in Egypt, in an attempt to resolve the ongoing Suez Canal crisis.

About this time, I had decided that a career in agriculture was not for me.

An advert in the Readers Digest had caught my attention. It was for the Fleet Air Arm, who were looking for pilots and navigators. I applied, and was duly asked to attend at RAF Hornchurch in Essex, for Flying Aptitude tests in January 1957. So when my dairy farm stint finished in late December I turned my back on farming, without much regret, and looked forward to the exciting new challenge that 1957 would present.

I reported to RAF Hornchurch in late January; after a long overnight train journey from Inverness, through a snow clad countryside. Some thirty nine of us Fleet Air Arm hopefuls had assembled for the tests. We had to undergo a three day course of written tests and cockpit simulation sessions so as to determine our suitability. In the end, only two were deemed to have passed–an Irish chap in his mid twenties, whose father owned a bar in Dublin and myself!

We were issued with travel warrants, and told to proceed to a Fleet Air Arm base in Gosport near Portsmouth, for commissioning tests. We travelled up to London, where my Irish companion worked out the train times, and decided that we could spend most of the day in London, before catching a connection to Gosport in the late afternoon. He decided that we should celebrate our success in passing stage one, and to this end, we embarked on a tour of Soho hostelries, drinking Guinness like it was going out of fashion.

My Irish companion had clearly been weaned on his native brew, and I made the mistake in trying to match him, drink for drink. It was a big mistake. Caught in the grip of severe alcohol poisoning, I remember very little of the train journey to Portsmouth, and even less of the short ferry trip across to Gosport. Next day my Irish drinking companion told me that the old matelot in charge of the ferry boat had seen me hanging over the boat rail. On being told that I was sea sick, and a potential Fleet Air Arm officer, the old salt nearly burst a blood vessel. He had never seen anybody sea sick on a short harbour crossing before, and despaired for this modern Navy, and the types it was now attracting.

Next morning I could not look at the breakfast served to us in the Mess. There was to be no respite as commissioning tests followed right away and certainly no allowance made for my wretched and hung-over condition. Mid morning I found myself facing an arc of six Naval officers each one seemed to be sporting more gold braid than the other. I was asked various questions, and soon my superficial knowledge of the Navy, the Fleet Air Arm and things aeronautical was to be cruelly exposed.

The Chairman of the group–the one who wore most gold braid, and to whom the other Board members treated with some deference–asked me for my views on angled flight decks, that had just been introduced to aircraft carriers. I had not got the faintest idea what he was talking about, and decided to bluff it out. I held forth about how the decks were angled, so as to provide a ramp effect to help slow down fast approaching aircraft attempting a deck landing. It seemed a logical answer to his question at the time. The wry smiles, and exchanged glances among the Board members made me realise that I was on the wrong track. The look on the Chairman's face was one of total disbelief. He slowly steepled his fingers in front of him, and after a long studied silence remarked: "How ingenious. Somebody should inform the Admiralty!"

From then on it was all downhill, and it came as no surprise to learn, at the end of the day, that I had not passed. My Irish companion fortified by Guinness had passed. He wanted me to wait overnight to help him celebrate his success, but I found this invitation very easy to decline!

I made the long train journey back to Inverness, somewhat depressed but the natural optimism of youth soon dispelled that.

A family friend, Jack Mackenzie, a former wartime commando who owned a small contracting business, took me on as a temporary labourer, while I considered my options. This was decided for me, as National Service beckoned, because my university deferment had by now ceased.

The expected letter arrived, asking me to attend for medical and registration at the Northern Meeting Rooms in Church Street, Inverness. The Meeting Rooms was a building of some distinction and tradition–I say was, as it was torn down, like so many old Inverness landmarks in the sixties, in the name of "progress". The building was really two ballrooms, one on the ground floor, and one on the first floor, with various smaller rooms for other purposes. Every September it was the venue for the Northern Meeting Ball. This was an all night dance, ending with breakfast and beer and was the social highlight of the Highland season for the kilted estate owners, and a lesser variety of social climbers. Royalty, in the shape of Princess Margaret had been known to attend the event.

Outwith the social season, the Meeting Rooms were hired out for a variety of purposes, one being as the National Service registration point. A local dance entrepreneur would also hire it to run weekend dances for the young folk of the town. The upstairs ballroom would feature old time dancing to a Scottish dance band, and downstairs modern dancing to satisfy the rapidly emerging rock and roll generation. Indeed, some three years later in early 1960, the attraction at the modern dancing was the appearance of the current Top Twenty singing star called Johnny Gentle. Backing him was an obscure Liverpool group called the Silver Beatles. When last heard of, Johnny Gentle was an unemployed plasterer in his native London East End, while the Silver Beatles dropped the metallic content from their name, and played their way into popular music history.

So it was to this venerable institution, that I assembled along with fifty to sixty other Inverness youths for National Service registration. The morning passed doing various written tests and about noon, we broke up for lunch and were told to report back at 2pm sharp, for the medical side of the business. I had bumped into a fellow shinty player from Newtonmore and tagged along with him and some of his friends as we went on our break. We crossed the street, and went down the narrow close to the back bar of the Gellions Hotel, a well known Inverness watering hole. Over the next hour over a few games of darts, we quaffed several pints of lager while discussing the iniquity of National Service.

Reporting back at 2pm as ordered, we were met by a short, balding Medical Corps Corporal who split us into groups of eight. We had to strip off to our underpants to pass through the various medical tests by different doctors. The Corporal handed our batch a small glass specimen flask, and we had to write our name on the white label attached. This done, he led us to a small servery room, and left us to the task of producing a urine sample. Somewhat self consciously, we all started to the task in hand. No sooner had I moved smoothly into action, than I realised that drink was about to play yet another part in my young life. My bladder was full to bursting with the unaccustomed intake of lunch time lager and no way was this small flask going to contain all that I had to offer.

I looked round in desperation and caught sight of an empty milk bottle standing by the servery counter. I grabbed it and managed what I thought was a reasonably slick transfer, as the specimen flask threatened to brim over.

I ended up with a full specimen flask in my left hand, a three quarter full milk bottle in my right, while standing barefoot in a small spreading puddle. Next to me was a pimply youth from the Western Isles. I am not sure whether he was simply unable to produce a specimen or if the sound and sight of my veritable Niagara had caused his bladder to seize up with some form of urinary inferiority complex. Seeing his plight, I offered to top up his flask from my milk bottle overflow, but he refused my generous gesture. He backed away from me with a savage shaking of his head and muttering something darkly in Gaelic.

The look on the Corporal's face when he came to claim our flasks, will live long in my memory.

The rest of the induction process passed without mishap. We had now reached the point of deciding which branch of the Services, and what unit we would join to see out our service period. A form was given to us, and on it we had to list three choices in order of preference.

Sergeant Groves, who was in charge was quite up front with us. He informed us that as humble National Servicemen the choice did not lie with us, and we could be put wherever there were vacancies.

The listing of choices was therefore worthless, and presented me with a very real problem. Elder brother Gerry had completed his National Service in 1956. He had joined the local Regiment, the Cameron Highlanders and as luck would have it, enjoyed two ideal years. After basic training, he had gone to the Edinburgh Tattoo for a summer season as part of the Regiment's military dancing team. In the autumn he and the rest of the dancing troupe set off to join the battalion in Lunenberg in Germany. From there, the battalion took off for Korea to assist in mopping up operations in the wake of the Korean War. A two week leave period in Tokyo was thrown in before the Camerons cruised home through the Indian Ocean, the Red Sea and the Mediterranean to reach the United Kingdom and demobilisation.

Since then the Camerons had been a fixture in the Redford Barracks in Edinburgh, and it would be just my luck to join them, and be stuck in the capital for the duration. I dare not leave it to chance because I still, at that time, harboured thoughts of applying again for the Fleet Air Arm, after my National Service period.

A poster on the wall caught my eye. It declaimed "IT'S A MAN'S LIFE IN THE GLIDER PILOT REGIMENT"–and down below in smaller print, "And The Parachute Regiment". But I was not into reading small print. Glider Pilot!–what a perfect solution to my problem– to do my National Service and at the same time gain valuable flying experience to boot.

In the event, it did not turn out to be as straight forward as all that. The offer was only open to regular soldiers and not to National Servicemen. To become a regular, one had to sign on for a minimum of three years. On the plus side, one would be paid, as at regular rates instead of National Service pittance. What was one more year I thought to myself–in for a penny in for a pound!

The die was cast. I signed on the dotted line and accepted the Queen's Shilling.

Some weeks later I was informed by letter that the Glider Pilot Regiment had disbanded to form the Army Air Corps. This Corps did not exist at this moment in time, so I was headed for better or worse into the open arms of the Parachute Regiment........

****

The train jolted to a stop and roused me from my reverie. Glancing out of the window I saw the station sign for Aldershot and below it a larger sign "WELCOME TO ALDERSHOT–HOME OF THE BRITISH ARMY".

This was it–I had arrived!

CHAPTER 3

ALDERSHOT
THE ARRIVAL

Thursday 11th July 1957

> I didn't raise my boy to be a soldier
> I brought him up to be my pride and joy
> Who dares to put a rifle on his shoulder
> To shoot another mother's darling boy?
>
> World War 1 ditty.

I emerged blinking into the strong afternoon sunlight after the relative gloom of the railway station.

Maida Barracks–now how do I find my way there?

A group of taxi drivers in shirt sleeves were standing smoking and chatting beside the taxi rank. Clutching my heave suitcase and with my raincoat draped over my arm I approached them. One of them straightened up and put out his cigarette at the prospect of a fare paying customer.

"How do I get to Maida Barracks?" I queried.

I reckon at this point the taxi driver realised that I was not going to be a client and his interest level waned considerably.

"You joining the Paras, mate? Take my advice and desert now while you've still got the chance!"

The group of taxi drivers dissolved into general laughter.

Eventually one of them gave me directions. He told me to proceed up the street facing me as far as the NAAFI Club, then turn left and when I had reached the cinema I would find a road called Hospital Hill which would lead me directly to Maida Barracks.

I set off following his instructions and just before the NAAFI Club I stopped to change hands on my suitcase. A sign in a theatre ticket agency window caught my eye, or at least the name Agatha Christie did. The poster was advertising an Agatha Christie play called "The Mousetrap"–now in its 5th Great Year in some London theatre. In my suitcase was an

Agatha Christie novel "The Murder of Roger Ackroyd" that I had bought in Inverness station to pass the long train journey.

But 5th Great Year–how could a play last that long in the same theatre and surely everybody in the world had seen it by now!

I carried on following the directions given to me. Aldershot, or what I had seen of it so far, seemed to be a well laid out township and not quite what I had expected. Somehow I had imagined a large Army camp and little else. Knowing that I was coming to Aldershot I had done some research in the Inverness library. In 1854 Aldershot was set up as a military community when a hutted and tented camp had been set up in some 25,000 acres of common heathland. It was an ideal base for conducting nineteenth century European warfare.

It also suited the officer classes in those early days. They were able to pursue their hunting activities as well as attending the London social scene and all this interspersed with some part-time soldiering. In 1881 Aldershot took on a more permanent look as brick built barracks were constructed and since then various armed conflicts had confirmed its status as the Home of the British Army.

What a colourful sight Aldershot must have presented in the days before the 1st World War. The variety of troops, in their distinctive uniforms, as they marched or walked through the town. Hussars in their braided jackets and busbies, Dragoons with their scarlet tunics and gleaming helmets, Lancers in coloured plastron tunics and plumed caps and the universal scarlet tunics and spiked helmets of the Infantry of the Line. Now the more serviceable khaki uniforms brought a somewhat drab uniformity to reflect changing times.

I found Hospital Hill and it inclined to higher ground overlooking the town. At the top was Cambridge Military Hospital and beyond a range of barrack blocks all built with a dull red brick denoting the original early Victorian building.

I came across Maida Barracks almost immediately and reported to the Guardroom where my details were checked. A corporal then conducted me in silence through the lines to a barrack block. We entered and I found myself in a large room with about forty to fifty beds laid out with a tall metal locker beside each bed. The room was deserted. "Wait here" said my corporal escort. "Just grab an empty bed space and the rest will be back shortly".

With that terse instruction he departed, leaving me to kick my heels. I heaved my suitcase on to the first available empty bed. Most of the other beds were blanketed and clearly in use, but at least three other spaces were still available. Within ten minutes the corporal returned with quite clearly another recruit. A dark haired chap with a sallow complexion and bad teeth who turned out to be a fellow Scot from Glasgow called Maclean.

He claimed another bed space and we chatted while we waited for further developments. Suddenly the room was crowded and noisy as the rest of the recruits returned. In charge of them was another corporal clutching a mill board.

"Who the hell are youse two?" he demanded of us looking hard at the typewritten names on his mill board. We identified ourselves. "Bloody latecomers" grumbled the corporal as he added our names in pen to the bottom of his typed name sheet. This simple act was to haunt Maclean and myself for the duration of our training as all names had been typed in strict alphabetical order on his sheet–except for us two!

The corporal informed us that we were now members of 124 Platoon of Recruit Company, the Parachute Regiment.

Apparently every two weeks a Platoon of recruits was formed to commence their ten weeks basic infantry training combined with a strict fitness regime to see if they were suitable material to join Airborne Forces. The addition of our names meant that 124 Platoon now numbered forty eight aspirants to the Parachute Regiment. 124 Platoon would commence formal training on Monday 15th July so we had the weekend to settle into our new way of life. Maclean and I were taken off to some store to draw necessary bedding material. As we made up our beds I had a chance to observe my fellow recruits. They seemed to be in every shape and size and the variety of accents was quite amazing. Many of them had arrived earlier in the week and had been issued with their Army uniforms while others were still in their civilian clothes. The ones in Teddy boy drape suits and winklepicker shoes cut an incongruous figure in the starkness of the billet room. We followed the others into the dining hall for supper. It was packed and noisy with some two hundred others queuing for food and then sitting at long tables. After supper we retired to our billet to unpack our suitcases and store items in the tall metal locker at our bedside. The recruit in the next bed to me, with all the authority of somebody who had been in the Army for three days, advised me to keep my locker secured at all times as things had a habit of going missing.

And so to bed–as I lay there I wondered how many countless thousands of other soldiers had spent their first night in this very billet. It was not long before sleep claimed me especially after the broken sleep of the previous night on the overnight train from Inverness. And so ended my first day in the Army.

Next morning after breakfast our corporal put in an appearance. His name I learned was Cpl Meredith and he would be with us for the duration of our training. Our Platoon Sergeant was to be a Sgt Sharman, who had seen action in the ill fated Suez campaign. He would meet with us later in the day. This being Friday, those of us who had still not been issued with our Army gear were taken to the Quartermaster's stores before it closed for the weekend. We filed past a large counter as storemen briskly issued us with all the equipment that we would need to see us through training. We trailed back to our billet weighed down with our newly issued Army gear. Cpl Meredith had by now acquired two assistants by the names of Hunter and Williams. They bore one chevron on their uniform and were lance-corporals and sometime referred to as lance-jacks.

We sat on our beds looking bemused at the equipment we had just been issued with. Cpl Meredith then demanded our attention.

"Listen your shower! Over this weekend it is our job to help you settle into the Army before basic training starts properly on Monday. Now, we fully appreciate that it will come as a f***ing shock to many of you nancy boys, but we are unshockable as you will soon find out. At this stage we look on you as new born babes and if you like we are sort of maternity nurses. We will teach you everything–and I mean every f***ing thing!– how to stand, walk, dress, use the toilet–the lot. Starting with how to make your bed and lay out your locker Army style".

He was as good as his word. All items of kit were held up, we were told what its use was, how to clean and how to present it for a locker inspection. All civilian clothes were to be stored away in our suitcases below our beds and we had to change into uniform. At last we were all dressed alike in army shirt, denim trousers, gaiters and boots all topped off with the famous red beret complete with silver wing badge. It did not seem to please Cpl Meredith who snorted in derision "You look like Fred Karno's bloody army!"

As a last touch L/Cpl Hunter handed out red tabs to each of us. We were told that we had to wear them at all times on the epaulettes of our shirt. One of the recruits asked the reason for this.

"This is to identify you wingless wonders as the lowest form of life crawling round this Depot–and don't you forget it!" responded Meredith. Referring once more to his ever present mill board he proceeded to give us our Army numbers. In my case it was 23525694. This number had to be written or sewn on every conceivable piece of equipment and stamped onto such items as mess tins.

We broke for lunch and as we entered the dining hall we were met with a sudden chorus of catcalls and whistles from the other diners. In truth we must have looked a real motley crew.

After lunch we were taken to see a film called 'For Theirs was the Glory' about the Arnhem campaign–Operation Market Garden. The Parachute

Regiment, despite being the youngest regiment in the British Army had forged a fine reputation and the ill fated assault on the Arnhem Bridge during World War 2 was widely regarded as their finest hour.

When the film show was over it was decided to pass the rest of the afternoon with a game of football.

We changed into red PT vests and shorts and plimsolls for this event. We were taken in a group to a nearby recreation area and divided into two teams about twenty four-a-side! In order to differentiate between the two teams, one team divested themselves of their PT vests and one side retained them. One team was called "Vests" and the other team "Skins" while the discarded PT vests were used to make temporary goals. I ended up in the "Skins" team. What followed was a highly enjoyable game of kick and rush football with very little scope for any real skill. The game was refereed by a newcomer–a very athletic looking individual in tight track suit bottoms and striped jersey top. He sported a severe crew cut and we soon learned that he was a Physical Training Instructor (PTI) and his name was Cpl Grogan. He would be looking after our fitness interests during our basic training.

All too soon the game was over as the final whistle blew shrilled and Grogan yelled at us to get into three lines, and make it fast. The "Skins" team members made a headlong dash to reclaim their PT vests. I strolled over and found that only one PT vest remained. When I tried to put it on I found that in the rush to claim vests somebody had taken my vest–and that person had to be the smallest recruit in our Platoon! The PT vest that I held was too small. The vest had a tight circular collar and try as I might my head could not go through it. By this time I was standing in line with the rest, still wrestling with the PT vest. I was aware of Cpl Grogan watching me closely and the muffled laughter from my fellow recruits at my plight.

"What the f***k's the matter with you?" growled Grogan, now standing facing me. I thought it was only too obvious what was the matter, but I decided to play it safe.

"It's this PT vest Sir, it's too small" I volunteered. Grogan's voice climbed several decibels. "Don't call me f***king Sir!–you bloody crow. What did your last f****ing nanny die of?" The PT vest all this time was nestling on top of my head like a turban with my attempts to put it on. Grogan suddenly grabbed the vest in both hands and pulled down violently. There was a sudden rending of material and I only just managed to restrain myself from checking if my ears were still attached to my head. The mutilated vest ended up round my neck. "There you are– f****ing fits now, don't it?" declared Grogan well pleased with his handiwork while the Platoon laughter was a ready chorus. We then jogged back to the billet, a solid mass of soldiers all dressed alike–except for me with the torn vest still round my neck. During this run back, Grogan appeared loping easily at my side. "You!–yes you foreskin features–what's your f****ing name anyway?" "Grant, Si...Corporal" I responded. Grogan absorbed this information. "Training starts proper on Monday and if you last the first week it will be classed as a f****ing miracle!"

With that parting shot he loped off to the head of the squad. As we approached the billet Sgt Sharman was waiting for us. He cut an impressive figure by any standards. His tall lean figure was ram rod straight as he eyed our approach expressionless.

He was in shirt sleeve order, with immaculate knife edge creases in both his shirt and trousers. His highly polished boots glistened and a vivid red sash was draped bandolier fashion across his chest while he clutched in his hand a pace stick.

We clattered to an untidy halt in front of him and waited for him to speak. This was the man who was to be in charge of us for our ten weeks of training. He continued to look at us without speaking and an uncomfortable silence developed. His gaze eventually settled on me, which was not difficult, as I was standing in the front row with the offending PT vest still draped round my neck.

Sgt Sharman jabbed his pace stick in my direction and turned to Cpl Grogan with an unspoken look of enquiry. Grogan in turn shrugged his shoulders and tapped the side of his forehead with his fingers as if to indicate a mental defective.

This wordless pantomime completed, Sharman turned again to face us. As his eyes swept over us again, his face darkened, his mouth tightened and his hand on the pace stick kept clutching and unclutching as if to suppress some inner turmoil. The silence dragged on and then at last he spoke. "Jesus wept gently!" he ground out then abruptly turned on his heel and strode away.

We stood our ground nonplussed.

Cpl Meredith chortled. "When the Serge quotes the f****ing Bible then you are in big trouble. I somehow get the feeling that he's not too impressed with you lot!" FALL OUT!"

And so ended our first full day in the Army and for many of us it was proving a tough baptism.

Saturday morning we once more paraded after breakfast to be met by Cpl Meredith and his inevitable mill board.

He marched us up to a small wooden hut and we stood there in three ranks. Cpl Meredith consulted his mill board. "Anybody here done art in school?" he enquired. Anxious to get back into anybody's good books, I raised my hand along with another recruit.

"Right, you two–come with me" and he led us into the hut.

Inside the hut were two barber's chairs with two barbers busy laying out the tools of their trade.

"O.K. you two artists. You said that you could handle a brush" said Meredith laughing as he handed us two floor brushes. "Well, your job is to keep the floor clear of hair clippings".

The two barbers were civilians who clearly were entrusted with the recruit Company contract. The head barber was a small man with a white tunic jacket buttoned up to his neck with a permanent Woodbine cigarette attached to his mouth. The Woodbine was allowed to smoulder away and never removed until it was time to light up another. 124 Platoon recruits came in two at a time. The head barber would slip a protective sheet round the recruits neck and carefully tuck it in. As he adjusted the height of the chair he would ask "And how would Sir like his hair done?"

The recruit in the chair, pleasantly surprised, would proceed in most cases to give lengthy and explicit instructions as to how to treat his crowning glory. The barber would then proceed to give the recruit a regulation short back and sides and some minutes later a shorn recruit would stumble out of the chair rather like a sheep having had its fleece removed. When the haircuts were completed they left by another door to return to the billet so that the ones waiting had no idea what was in store for them. As we wielded our brushes we were entertained by the ongoing comedy as the barber would ask each recruit the same question and then tear into them with the same end result. We were kept pretty busy as carefully cultivated and expensively maintained "Tony Curtis" hair styles and Teddy Boy quiffs were deposited on the bare linoleum floor for our attention.

As the last recruit vacated the chair it was our turn. As I sat in the chair and had the sheet tucked round my neck I caught the barber's eye in the mirror as he was about to pose the usual question to me. "Don't even bother!" I said and thought I detected a faint smile on his face as he bent to his work.

When we two shorn would-be artists returned to our billet we were once more paraded outside and to our surprise Sgt Sharman appeared as immaculate as ever. This time he spoke to us.

"Right–Look in you lot. My name is Sgt Sharman and for better or worse I will be your Platoon Sergeant. Yesterday the sight of you lot was quite frankly unnerving–I had to go home and lie down in a darkened room. However, I have a job to do and it is to see you lot through ten weeks of basic training". Here he consulted his mill board.

"Now the Platoon numbers forty eight bodies. What I can tell you here and now–no way will forty eight of you complete the course far less be accepted into the Parachute Regiment. It's a hard fact of life that roughly only 20% of any Platoon will pass. There is no quota system. If none of you are up to it then none of you will pass–simple as that. The rest of the British Army have to accept the recruits that they get and knock them into shape as best they can. The Paras are different–we select very carefully those whom we consider suitable to serve with us–that is what makes us the elite fighting force in this man's Army. Is that understood?" "Yes, Serge" we choroused.

Sharman continued "You will find the next ten weeks reasonably soul searching and you will be monitored and observed at all times. We will take you apart to see what makes you tick and then put you back together again. Some of you may never be put back as you were and from what I can see of most of you then that will be no bad thing! You will not be wet nursed as that is in nobody's interests. You either have it or you haven't. Now training commences properly on Monday and over the weekend the Corporals will help you sort out your equipment. That's all!" And with that he marched off.

We were left with plenty to think about as we fell out to await Monday and the start of basic training.

CHAPTER 4

124 PLATOON
1st WEEK TRAINING

15th July–21st July 1957

> For we have come from schoolrooms
> To learn the fighting trade;
> So that we, the Young in Summers
> Will know the Rules Experience made.
>
> Anon.

Monday morning dawned 15th July 1957. Reveille was at 6 a.m. sharp. I was so used to rising at 5 a.m. for my farm duties that I was the only one up and about. Around me in the early morning half light were sleeping bodies and the sound of snoring. 6 a.m. brought the Corporals shouting and beating a noisy alarm on the wall with a mess tin.

"WAKEY! WAKEY! Right hands off c**ks–and hands on socks!" was their cheery shouted greeting. The rest of the Platoon struggled into life and then queued to wash and shave. The first item on our agenda was a trip to Maida Gym suitably attired in PT kit. I had obtained another properly sized PT vest by this time and had been told that the cost of the old ruined vest would be deducted from my first pay packet.

Waiting at the Gym for us was Cpl Grogan.

He wasted no time. "Right you lot–the fun starts here! Welcome to Maida Gym where you are going to lose a lot of blood and sweat over the next few weeks as we knock your evil bodies into some sort of shape. Here, there is no hiding place as you will find out. How you perform will go a long way to seeing if you are cut out to be a Para. We will not wait until the end of the course to fail you–if at any stage we see you are not up to it– you will be binned–O.K.–no messing!"

To my embarrassment his gaze fixed on me.

"You–what's your name again .....Grant–Yes that's it. One day in the bloody army and you go about sabotaging Army equipment. Where on earth do they drag you swine up from? Anyway I wouldn't have thought it worth your while getting a new vest for if you survive the first week I'll be a f****ing Dutchman!"

The Platoon gave him a round of relieved laughter.

He next turned his attention to the diminutive figure of Ray Haddon in the front row.

"You–what f****ing size are you? Christ, if you ever parachute a strong breeze will carry you away!"

More Platoon laughter, in which I joined in, glad that I was not the only butt of his twisted sense of humour.

The next thirty minutes were spent jogging, sprinting, doing press-ups and climbing wall bars and ropes. At the end we were told that the first light warming up session was over and so to breakfast.

We then had to get dressed for early morning parade. When we lined up in three ranks outside the billet Sgt Sharman and his mill board took over. He consulted his list of names and started a roll call.

When his name was called out the recruit in question had to stand to attention and repeat his name and army number. Halfway through this recital he called out "GREENWOOD" and received no response. Greenwood had disappeared in the night, complete with his suitcase, leaving no farewell message or forwarding address.

Sgt Sharman on learning of this commented sourly–"If I had to start training with you lot–I'd probably have done the same!"

He carried on and a few names later he called out "LOCKHART" and again no response. It was left to Cpl Meredith to inform him that the civilian Police had called on Sunday and Lockhart had been taken away for questioning. The Police could not give details but had advised Cpl Meredith not to expect Lockhart's speedy return to military duties–if at all!

When he had at last completed the roll call, Sharman exploded.

"Bloody hellfire! We haven't even started the first bloody day and we are minus two bodies already. This must be some kind of f****ing record in Airborne history!"

We were then subject to an intense personal scrutiny and all manner of defects were pointed out to us. These ranged from how we were dressed to matters of personal hygiene like shaving and cleanliness of finger nails. In no uncertain terms we were told that for the first week we would not be allowed near the square until we had achieved some semblance of looking and marching like soldiers. Sharman wanted us to see the other Platoons marching on to parade so that we would know the future form. There were currently three Platoons ahead of us in the system. 123 Platoon, immediately ahead of us were commencing their third week–122 Platoon were on their 6th week while 121 Platoon were on their ninth and penultimate week.

We stood, highly impressed, watching these Platoons marching down through the lines to go on parade with their Platoon Sgts at their side barking out commands.

When the last Platoon had passed Sharman turned to us.

"Can anybody tell me about any important fact that strikes you as these other Platoons marched past?"

One or two hopeful suggestions were put forward until one of our recruits called Roly Gamble hit the mark.

"The Platoons are getting smaller in numbers, Serge!"

"Smack on!" said Sharman, clearly satisfied that he had got the answer he was looking for. "That is all part of the culling process that takes place with every Platoon as they progress through basic training. 121 Platoon are almost on their final week and they now number twenty four down from an original starting point of about sixty."

Sharman suddenly stiffened to attention. A lone figure came into view heading in the direction of the square.

He was a thick set individual with a ruddy complexion that went well with the red beret on his head. Instead of a sash he sported a highly polished leather belt across his chest and his massive fist gripped a large pace stick.

On seeing us he stopped.

"Sgt Sharman—is this your new Platoon?"

"Yes, Sir" replied our Platoon Sgt. standing rigidly to attention.

"Well, by the look of them, you are going to have your work cut out and no mistake!" With that parting shot he swaggered off in the direction of the square. Sharman visibly relaxed and glanced down at his mill board. "I see from this that most of you are Church of England, with five Catholics and no less than three atheists. Well, I have news for you three unbelievers—you have just seen GOD! He has come back on earth in the shape of RSM (Regimental Sergeant-Major) Duffy, and if you take my advice, do not cross his path during your stay here."

When the Depot morning parade was over we were taken down to the now deserted square. Our morning was filled with our first drill session. We were taught how to stand to attention, stand at ease, march as a group and how to come to a halt, not forgetting how to execute a salute. During this session I found a certain problem starting to affect me. In the week before leaving for the army I had played my last league game for Kirkhill Football Club. In the course of the match I received a kick in the thigh and had to be taken off. The immediate pain soon disappeared and, although I was left with a bruised and discoloured thigh, I soon forgot about it. However, the prolonged drill session had caused my leg muscle to knot up and become quite painful. As I limped off the square L Cpl Hunter spotted this and told me if it was no better by the next day that I should report sick. I would then be back squadded and once my leg had cleared I would then join a later Platoon. I found the thought that I would be the third person to fall out of 124 Platoon quite depressing.

In the afternoon we were introduced to the Confidence Course which would play a very prominent part in our training. The Course was set in a wooded area just off the Queens Avenue road leading to Farnborough. It consisted of a circuit of obstacles designed to test to the utmost our stamina, fitness and ability to operate with confidence at certain heights. Each and every obstacle was explained to us in some detail and we were shown the approved way to tackle them.

Tomorrow would be our first crack at the course. My leg was really giving me some discomfort at this stage and I knew in my heart that tackling the course with it in this condition would be well nigh impossible.

Once back in the billet I voiced my fears and one of the other recruits called Blyth said he would take a look at my thigh. After a cursory look at it he declared that it was no problem and that he had the very stuff for it. He went over to his bed space and dug into his suitcase to emerge with a deep metal tin. He prised the lid off to reveal that it was half filled with a dark, brown greasy ointment.

"What the hell is this stuff?" I asked with understandable suspicion.

Blyth assured me that he knew exactly what he was doing and proceeded to smear the stuff on my thigh and massage it in quite firmly. There was no real smell from the ointment for which I was grateful, so it was with a somewhat greasy thigh but still somewhat depressed that I went to bed that night. I awoke in the middle of the night with a start! My thigh was not only sore–it was pulsing and felt as if my leg was on fire. I shot out of bed and hobbled as best I could to the toilet area where I attempted to run cold water over my inflamed limb. I cursed my stupidity in even allowing Blyth, who had no real medical experience that I knew of, to have even looked at my leg. After what seemed ages I crept back to my bed resisting the strong temptation to deliver a kick to Blyth's recumbent body as I passed his bed.

I lay awake for a long time after that aware of my aching thigh and the realisation that I would have to go sick first thing in the morning. About 4 a.m. I eventually drifted off into sleep. In the morning, when I finally came to–I could not believe it! My leg no longer ached and there was no pain or restriction of movement. I felt such a surge of relief that I realised how some poor unfortunate cured at Lourdes must feel like.

At breakfast, as the more advanced Platoons catcalled, I slipped alongside Blyth in the breakfast line to tell him about his miracle cure. He took my good news quite calmly.

"I knew it would do the trick. Before I was called up for National Service I worked in the racing stables at Newmarket. We used to use the stuff all the time on the horses whenever they went lame with a sprain!"

He moved on in the queue and I was left open mouthed at this revelation. Word got round about my 'miracle' cure and later one of the other recruits approached me. He had pulled a muscle in his groin and could I recommend Blyth's ointment for him. I asked him if at any time in the future did he ever plan to get married and have children. A bit puzzled he replied in the affirmative so I advised him to steer well clear of Blyth and let nature take its course with his groin strain.

My leg not only stood up to the morning drill session, but allowed me to tackle the Confidence Course as well. Indeed I felt like something akin to a racehorse myself as I sped round the course happily relieved that the spectre of back squadding had been well and truly lifted.

Every night after supper a routine was developed called 'Shining Hour'. It ran from 7 p.m. to 8 p.m. and during this hour we had to prepare our kit for the next day. We ironed trousers and shirts, blancoed belts and gaiters and wielded brasso like it was going out of fashion.

Our second or best pair of boots came in for special treatment. Firstly, we had to burn off the dimpled leather on the toe-cap and heel so that it became a flat surface. Then literally, with spit and polish we had to work boot polish into the boot until it gleamed. This process could take many hours to achieve the accepted highly polished end result.

During this hour we were not allowed to speak and Sharman or the Corporals constantly patrolled to ensure this. So we resembled a monastic order of monks as we toiled away in total silence at our bedspaces.

Anybody who broke the silence was punished with fifty press-ups.

In the bed space next to mine was a recruit called Green from Birmingham whom everybody called Brummy. He was about my height but much thicker set. He informed us that his main hobby was body building and that he had won medals in his class at various national competitions. We could well believe this as his upper body was very well developed. As it was summer time everybody worked stripped to the waist in the billet.

When "Shining Hour" was over, Brummy would settle down to his exercises before an admiring audience. He would grasp his hands in front of his body and his upper body seemed to swell to double its size as dormant muscles rippled and bulged. It was, by any standards, an impressive spectacle and I felt a bit like the original seven stone weakling by comparison. Sharman came back one night and quietly observed Brummy's floor show.

He ordered me to stand alongside Brummy and then remarked to the Platoon "If we can get Grant and half of the rest of you to look anything like Green by the end of training, I'll be satisfied."

It is remarks like that that can sap one's morale and the sight of Green's smirk as he accepted Sharman's back handed compliment.

Next morning, instead of our Maida Gym session we were told to report outside in PT vest, denim trousers and boots for a ten mile run. We set off running in a body with the three PTI's. Grogan and his two helpers snapping at our heels like demented terriers. We settled into a fast pace and about the three mile mark I saw Brummy who was just ahead of me start to falter and the tempo of his running become ragged. He is in trouble I thought. One of the PTI's also spotted this and ran alongside Brummy to give him some rough verbal encouragement. This seemed to work for a while, but gradually he started to falter and his breathing became laboured. About the five mile mark he suddenly swerved away from our ranks and collapsed in a heap by the roadside. Naturally we all slowed up, but Grogan appeared out of nowhere.

"LEAVE HIM ALONE!–Look to your front and keep running" he barked.

We completed the run and it was a hot, sweaty and steaming bunch of recruits that fell out back at the billet. We were ordered to get showered quickly before breakfast. In the billet Green's bed space was empty, and his vacant locker door swung ajar.

Cpl Meredith supplied the answer "Green's gone–turned out that he couldn't hack it. We don't allow people like that to hang around and pollute the place!"

We had little time to dwell on Green's demise as we were chased off to the showers.

Another recruit called Smith was sitting on his bed, clearly having some difficulty in removing his boot. He had one boot off and was taking the other boot off with a pained expression on his face. L/Cpl Williams stood by his bed shouting at him to get a move on. At last he removed his boot and the sole of his grey sock appeared blackened and matted. Even more gingerly Smith started to remove his sock and at this Williams lost his patience. He grabbed the sock and pulled it off violently. An unearthly scream knifed through the billet and everybody sort of froze.

Smith was writhing in agony on his bed with his hands covering his face uttering low groaning sounds. L/Cpl Williams stood by his bed equally shocked holding in his hand the sock with a very sizeable chunk of flesh from the sole of Smith's foot attached to it.

A jeep was hastily summoned and the luckless Smith was taken off to Cambridge Military Hospital nearby.

We were chased off to showers and breakfast as Depot life carried on. When we paraded, Sgt Sharman's roll call revealed that 124 Platoon had shed another two members–as Smith and Green, in Sharman's words, had both gone before breakfast!

Sharman took the opportunity to deliver a lecture to us on the importance of looking after ones feet. As infantrymen, it was our means of getting about and should never be neglected. It appeared that Smith had left a wrinkle in his sock when he put his boot on, and during the run this had cut into the soft flesh of his sole and caused the bleeding that made the sock adhere to the skin.

Everybody was experiencing blisters and minor foot damage to some extent and I gave thanks for the past year's farming and labouring that had toughened my feet.

That weekend some of us went to visit Smith in hospital and take along his personal gear. We found him sitting in a ward with his injured foot in a saline bath, reading a magazine. He told us that this treatment would continue for about ten days before they put a light cast on to help speed up his recovery.

To his credit, some twelve weeks later he was back-squadded to a later Platoon and eventually passed into the Parachute Regiment. That night after "Shining Hour", for a laugh, I stood where the late departed Green used to flex his over developed body and pretended to go through his routine. When the platoon laughter had subsided, nobody had observed Sharman standing quietly in the doorway who observed.

"O.K. Grant–every Platoon needs its f****ing comedian!"

During our first week, we all became aware of a shadowy figure who was at one stage introduced to us as Lt Ferguson, our Platoon Officer.

Meredith told us that he had served in Suez along with Sgt Sharman, but had been wounded in the action when a mortar shell explosion had mangled the fingers of his left hand. He was on the way out of the Army, but some complications over his financial compensation with the medical board had arisen, so he was passing time in Depot until the matter was resolved. One night towards the end of the first week he appeared at "Shining Hour" and decided to hold a foot inspection. We were all standing by our beds as he did his tour of inspection with L/Cpl Hunter in attendance. He paused by Colin Bateman's bed and picked up the boots Colin had been lovingly "bulling" up for days. Now Colin was the acknowledged Platoon expert at bulling boots. He achieved a shining gloss on his boots that nobody else seemed to be able to match.

Colin was, naturally, extremely proud of this God given talent. Lt Ferguson held up the boots and indeed they looked resplendent with the light gleaming and reflecting off them. Bateman stood by confidently waiting for the usual praise to be directed his way.

Ferguson said to one of the recruits "Put that bucket in the middle." Now in the centre of the room was a black leaded stove and alongside it a bucket to hold coal. Needless to say, the bucket had never seen coal and in fact was probably more highly polished now than on the day it was first made. Whittaker did as he was ordered, and placed the shining bucket in the middle of the floor. Ferguson then addressed us.

"I am going to leave the billet–and nobody must move for at least five minutes–is that understood?" We nodded assent.

With that he placed the boots in the bucket and bent over it so that we could not see what he was doing. He straightened up and strode smartly out of the billet. We stood as directed, perplexed and so did L/Cpl Hunter. There was suddenly a loud blast and a vivid flash from the bucket as it was blown sideways and Bateman's boots were blasted into the air amid a cloud of smoke. Lt Ferguson had slipped a thunderflash into the bucket alongside the boots. Thunderflashes were widely used on exercises to simulate the sound, and effect, of a thrown hand grenade.

When our initial shock had subsided, Colin sprang forward to reclaim his prized footwear. Then Lt Ferguson re-appeared in the billet doorway with a faint half smile on his face.

"Bateman" he called out "You're a bull shitting b*****d–get off to the bloody Guards who appreciate that kind of thing!"

He then left, but I doubt if Colin even heard his advice. He was standing by the overturned bucket cradling his still smoking and blasted boots in his cupped hands. It was the first time I had every seen anybody in deep and genuine shock. He stood there transfixed, saying over and over again in aggrieved tone "He blew me bloody boots up!"

By this time, most of us were doubled up with unkind laughter at Colin and the fate of his best boots.

We never saw our Platoon officer again. No doubt an equally stunned L/Cpl Hunter would have reported his eccentric behaviour to a higher power and that would have been that.

On Friday morning, our intensive drill periods had paid off as we were allowed to attend early morning parade in our own right.

We marched down to stand alongside Platoons 123, 122 and 121. First of all CSM (Company Sergeant Major) Banks stamped down the lines and snapped to attention before us. He checked each Platoon's dressing to see that the rows of men were dead in line. Then RSM Duffy swaggered onto the square and the parade proper began. Each Platoon Sgt had to bring us men up to attention and then report to the RSM that his particular Platoon was present and ready for his inspection.

The RSM conducted his inspection in great detail, complaining bitterly about every real and imagined shortcoming and demanding a higher standard of us on the next parade.

At last the ordeal was over and we got down to a morning of solid drilling. Before lunch we attended pay parade. This took the form of an officer sitting at a temporary table flanked by a pay clerk. We had to march up, come to attention, salute and present our Paybook. This book was duly recorded, the pay clerk handed us our money and, with a final salute, we turned away and marched back to the ranks. In my hot little hand was firmly clutched £5 three shillings and sixpence. It should have been really £5 ten shillings, but I had been deducted six shillings and sixpence for the PT vest that Cpl Grogan had mutilated on my first day.

In any event, it still beat the £1 fifteen shillings that brother Gerry got as his weekly National Service pay!

Our afternoon session on the Confidence Course was enlivened when one of our number, a recruit called Sharp, declared that he had had enough and was marched away by L/Cpl Hunter as the rest of us toiled round the circuit. We returned later to the billet to find yet another empty bed space where Sharp had been.

"Now I bloody well know what it must have been like for Battle of Britain pilots" said recruit Arthur Liles thoughtfully.

We all looked at each other in silence. Five down–who would be next? The culling had well and truly begun as our first week in training ended.

CHAPTER 5

REST OF BASIC TRAINING

July–September 1957

Thus we know the strength of armies
And the nature of the gun.
To have weight upon our shoulders
Before we're twenty-one!

Anon.

Monday 22nd July dawned bright and clear heralding the start of our second week of basic training.

Early morning roll call revealed yet another gap in our ranks. On the Sunday a recruit called Andrews from Brighton had taken a personal telephone call at the Guardroom and then had notified Cpl Meredith that his mother had died suddenly. He was immediately granted compassionate leave to go home and attend the funeral. We, naturally, extended our sympathies to him as he sadly packed his case before heading for home. The Orderly Room was duly informed and late on Sunday somebody contacted the Andrews household to get fuller details as the Depot Commanding Officer would be sending a telegram of sympathy next day. A lady answered the phone and identified herself as Andrew's mother and there had been most definitely no family bereavement! The military Police were then informed and the matter placed in their capable hands.

Sgt Sharman told us the details surrounding the loss of our latest Platoon member.

"To add insult to injury" he went on "I see that Andrews was one of the unholy trinity who declared themselves as atheists. So, now that he has clearly established beyond reasonable doubt that there is life after death–I am taking it upon myself to convert you other former unbelievers to C. of E.!"

With that he made the necessary adjustment on his mill board and the Christian faithful could boast of two more adherents.

It certainly kicked off Monday morning on a cheerful note.

Sharman looked sourly at his list of names and went on: "Week 1 is supposed to be a gentle introduction to this man's army. Yet, we're down no less than six recruits already. It's bloody well unheard of–by this rate there will be no Platoon left by Week 8 and the Corporals and myself can have a buckshee couple of weeks holiday. There's always a silver lining!".

We were soon left in no doubt that the screw was going to tightened. After roll call Sharman and his henchmen inspected our bed spaces with a fine tooth comb. Our beds were made up with blankets boxed at the head and all our personal gear laid out for inspection. Nobody escaped criticism and several beds were overturned to express displeasure at the standard of their display.

We were told in no uncertain terms to get things right for another inspection at 8 a.m. We passed muster at the second inspection, but in so doing had to miss out on breakfast. Then on to early morning parade where RSM Duffy vented his feelings on us. Life was getting no easier. About this time, the Platoon who until now had been forty individuals began to bond together not least as it seemed as if it was us against the rest of the world. Everybody else in Depot looked so assured, marching with purpose and looking the part in their uniforms complete with the blue parachute wings on their shoulders. Apart from us recruits.

Football was a subject of common interest to most recruits and the main subjects were the Busby Babes, the young Manchester United team that their Scottish Manager Matt Busby was grooming for stardom. Not to be outdone, Pearson from London who was a Chelsea supporter, was raving about a 17 year old player called Jimmy Greaves whom he reckoned would eclipse even Duncan Edwards the highly regarded United player.

I had become friendly with a couple of recruits who had joined up together. Henry Armstrong and John Wood known as Woody had been miners in their home town of Houghton-le-Spring in County Durham. They possessed rich Geordie accents and most of the southern English recruits found it hard to understand them.

One night at "Shining Hour" Woody started whistling as he polished his boots. Sgt Sharman seized on this breach of rules right away. "Right, Wood! If you think you are some kind of song bird you can entertain us all with a song."

To everybody's surprise Woody grabbed hold of the bumper that we used to polish the lino floor. Using it as a mock mike he gave out with a most professional rendering of "The Lady is a Tramp". Apparently, back home Woody was an accomplished performer in the local miners social club. Sgt Sharman had to grudgingly admit defeat, but still made Woody do press-ups just for good measure.

This had a sequel next day as we returned from another road run complete with full kit. As we neared Maida Barracks it was standard practice to march back into camp. As we slowed down to commence marching Sharman came alongside and said "O.K. let's march back to camp with a bit of style. Wood–give us a song that the rest can all join in.". Wood did as he was told and broke into a song–a song that was to become the theme song for 124 Platoon for the rest of our training.

> "It takes a worried man to sing a worried song:
> Oh, it takes a worried man to sing a worried song,
> It takes a worried man to sing a worried song,
> I'm worried now–but I won't be worried long"!

Up until now we had effectively been cut off from the rest of the world. We had seen no papers and there was not even a radio in the billet as we focussed at settling into army life. This was brought home to us one morning when at breakfast Roly Gamble informed us that Oliver Hardy the stout member of the film comedy duo Oliver and Hardy had died of a heart attack in America. One of the chefs doling out at the servery had told him.

The days began to slip past in a blur of activity as we moved into August. Drilling, marching, constant running, Maid Gym sessions, firing on the ranges and endless cleaning filled our waking hours. At the end of each day we crashed out and crawled into bed for a dreamless sleep that seemed all too short. We were now required to do three laps of the Confidence Course each time we visited it. It took further toll of our number when we lost two more recruits in the second week. One simply refused on a high piece of equipment and said that he had had enough. He was doubled away in quick time by L/Cpl Williams and yet another empty bed space awaited our return.

The other loss was not quite so straightforward.

On the Friday night of the second week, rain had fallen overnight and as a result some of the obstacles were down right dangerous. One in particular was an arrangement of large wooden sleeper type blocks built up to some 25/30 ft from the ground, designed to test our confidence to operate at a certain height. A recruit had to clamber to the top of this contraption, then run along a sleeper before leaping across a sizeable gap to land on another sleeper on the other side. Rain had the effect of making the take-off and landing sleeper quite slippery.

The inevitable happened. One recruit–it happened to be my personal quack medic Don Blyth–slipped on take off and crashed to the ground below. He lay there groaning and clutching what later turned out to be a broken ankle. As he lay there Grogan appeared as if out of nowhere and spotted the prostrate figure on the ground. "You! What the hell are you doing there–nobody told you to take a nap!" As Blyth groaned sunk in his personal misery, L/Cpl Hunter crouched beside him explained what had happened and that he had summoned a medic's jeep. "Right!" said Grogan, as he took this information on board–but he had a parting shot for the luckless Blyth. "Well, don't just f****ing lie there–do some press-ups!"

With these few words of solace he sped off shouting at some other recruits who were making heavy weather of the third circuit.

When we returned to the billet Sharman confirmed to us that Don had broken his ankle. As we fell out some wit remarked "Never mind, Don will soon be back as he's got some special ointment for that sort of thing!" There was much raucous laughter at this–but we were not to see Don back in the ranks of 124 Platoon that was now ending its second week reduced to forty in number.

We moved into the third week of our basic training. As we tucked into breakfast on Monday morning we spotted a sudden influx of about sixty new individuals in badly fitting denims and floppy berets. It was the rare sight of 125 Platoon on its first day! We subjected them to a noisy greeting of catcalls and booing as was their right.

Looking at these new recruits made us realise that we had come a long way in just two weeks.

By now we had reached a reasonable standard in our drilling.

Sgt Sharman now introduced us to something called 'cobwebbing'. This took the form of drill without rifles. We marched as usual in three compact ranks and at first the commands were called out in normal time. Then Sharman began to speed up the commands so that eventually they came one on top of another without a break. It was designed to make us concentrate and obey orders in quick time. However, after a time the Platoon fell into chaos as somebody turned right instead of left or reacted too slow to a command.

One morning we were engaged in this stimulating exercise and had fallen into the usual chaos. In fact the diminutive Ray Haddon had about turned too slowly and big John Evans had trampled him underfoot. The Platoon were halted to sort this situation out amid a certain amount of hilarity.

From the edge of the tree lined square came, what at first we thought, was a clap of thunder. Unknown to us, RSM Duffy had come quietly to the edge of the square to observe our debacle.

"Sgt Sharman! This Platoon is a bloody disgrace. Stand aside and I'll take them for a spell!" With that he strode over the square towards us and a ripple of real apprehension passed through our ranks.

Three times he brought us up to attention before he was satisfied. "STAND UP STRAIGHT!" he roared, pointing with his pace stick to one of the recruits on the front row. "You–Yes You!–the round shouldered individual at the end. Pull your shoulders back man and straighten your back. You look like a constipated vulture straining to have a crap!" With that we were off cobwebbing. At first all went well–QUICK MARCH–LEFT–RIGHT–LEFT–RIGHT TURN–ABOUT TURN until the RSM went into overdrive and soon the squad dissolved into a shambles with recruits marching blindly in all directions.

"HALT!" screamed Duffy–and we crashed to a stuttering halt. For some reason I ended up with my back to the RSM but face to face with my fellow Scot Maclean. We were practically rubbing noses and both of us panting into each other's face with our exertion. It was at this point that I discovered that Maclean in addition to having bad teeth also possessed breath that was not of the highest order! Nobody dared move a muscle.

The RSM's voice had by now risen, if it was possible, by several octaves. "My God! I have never seen anything like it in my life. You're spread round the square like a mad woman's shite!"

The RSM's obvious obsession with this particular bodily function and the mental picture that it conjured up was too much for me. I laughed out loud and then tried to kill it in mid air as I realised, too late, that I was a one man appreciation society. I closed my eyes for the wrath to come. "Get that hysterical Girl Guide off my square–NOW!" trumpeted Duffy. L/Cpl Hunter appeared at my elbow in a flash and mouthed "That means you pal!" as he whipped off my red beret.

We set off walking for the edge of the square.

"DOUBLE!–DOUBLE!" bellowed Duffy. "Double!" said Hunter and we fairly galloped off the square. We continued our run through the Depot lines and ended up at the Guardroom. Here I was booked in, put in a cell and the door slammed shut leaving me to my thoughts. That's really torn it I thought to myself, and imagined the rest of the Platoon returning to my empty bed space. I was somewhat cheered when some ten minutes later no less than two more of 124 Platoon joined me in the slammer.

"The RSM's going f****ing spare!" commented Evans morosely.

After an hour we were released from our stark surroundings and crept back into the billet not quite sure of what reception awaited us. The rest of the Platoon were getting ready for the Confidence Course and so we slipped back into the stream of things without much comment.

We were to realise later that RSM Duffy did his party piece on each new Platoon about their third week in order to concentrate their minds!" Maida Gym also took on a savage upturn in activity. We scaled ropes, wall bars, vaulted the wooden horse and sprinted round a gruelling indoor circuit course and in short lost sweat in every way known to man–or even a sadist like Cpl Grogan!

We spent long days on the firing ranges getting to fire and know the various weapons that we would use in battalion life. Somewhere along the line I qualified as a marksman on the bren gun.

The Platoon members had by now bonded well and several close friendships were forged. Sometime in the second week I had clashed with another recruit Arthur Liles from the London area. Some remarks were passed and ended up with us clashing physically only to be parted by other Platoon members. This was due to the fact that it would go against us if we were seen not to be getting on with Platoon members, in addition, any punishment meted out would affect the whole Platoon. As a result, any flare ups like this were quickly diffused.

After this confrontation, Liles and I tended to steer clear of each other. The end of the third week saw the August Bank holiday come about. Almost everybody with the exception of me were given a weekend pass and allowed to go home. I was left contemplating a solitary weekend in Maida barracks! I was pleasantly surprised when Liles came over to my bed space and said would I care to spend the weekend with his parents as opposed to staying in camp. Needless to say I readily accepted. So on the Friday night we caught the train to Surbiton, the bus to Kingston and then on to his home in Chessington. Mr and Mrs Liles, his parents, greeted me warmly and were both eager to hear about our first weeks in training. Over supper we had much to talk about and then at 6 p.m. his mother switched on the television to catch the evening news. It was the first time I had ever seen a television working as in 1957 TV reception had not yet come to the Highlands! The Liles thought this was hilarious as they had had a set every since the Queen's coronation in 1953 and it was now an accepted part of their every day life.

A most enjoyable weekend was spent after the strict military regime that we had endured. We went into Kingston and hung about the Kenya Coffee House. This Coffee House had large potted plants with green shrubbery so as to give the authentic jungle effect. It specialised in Espresso coffee with the inevitable juke box around which an interesting cross-section of Kingston girls used to congregate. Arthur Liles impressed me enormously with his ability to chat up members of the fairer sex. In fact, at the end of the evening he strolled off into the night with some girl he had been speaking to, saying blithely that he would see me back at the house.

Left on my own, I played the final selection of the juke box before I headed back to the Liles' residence in Chessington. The song I picked was

"Last Train to San Fernando" by Johnnie Duncan and the Blue Grass Boys–but for me it was a case of last bus to Chessington!

When we returned to the Depot after the weekend, I was chatting to Henry Armstrong about my visit to Chessington. I told him about the Coffee House saga and about Arthur Liles' uninhibited approach to chatting up and described him as a wolf. Little did I know then that I was to saddle Arthur 'Wolf' Liles with a nickname that would follow him throughout his Army career.

Now that we had completed four weeks in training we were allowed to go out into Aldershot at weekends, but only in uniform. This entailed reporting to the Guardroom to be inspected on the way out and to be back in camp by not later than 11 p.m. A group of us including Henry, Woody and Wolf used to go out in a group. Inevitably the first port of call was a pub and we used to favour the Rat Pit pub down by the NAAFI Club.

The two Geordies were dismayed to find that they could not get their Newcastle Brown Ale and had to make do with the local Courage bitter. This was most definitely not to their taste and they referred to it as 'Gnat's Piss'. As befitting ex-miners they could down pints with astonishing rapidity but I made sure that I never tried to reach their high standards.

By the end of week 4 we were down to thirty eight as two more recruits succumbed to foot injuries that necessitated them being back squadded until their injuries had healed.

Week 5 brought me a personal crisis. Sgt Sharman had declared himself unhappy with certain aspects of our drill and ordered us to parade for extra drill on the Saturday morning.

It started to rain so he took us to one of the empty MT (Motor Transport) sheds to get some shelter. This shed had a roof and a concrete floor, but otherwise was quite open to the elements.

We drilled for about an hour–shouldering, sloping and presenting arms. The constant slapping of the rifle butt into my cupped palm had caused a painful blue bruise to develop. As we shouldered arms for what seemed the umpteenth time the rifle butt slammed into my bruised palm causing me to flinch and drop the rifle with an almighty clatter. Sgt Sharman was round on me like a flash, red faced with anger and the pace stick right under my nose. "Grant–I've had enough of you! You can't even hold on to a bloody rifle". After the drill session finished I waited for the dreaded summons but nothing happened and I realised that I was, in a manner of speaking, still on course. As we commenced week 6 we were informed by Grogan that we had now reached the halfway point of our ten week course.

"Right 124 Platoon–or what's left of it! How many of your now–thirty eight chancers–and Grant what the hell are you doing hanging around like a bad smell for I just do not know. Still there's plenty of time left for them to get wise to you and some of you others as well. No names no pack drill!"

Then it was on to another punishing session in the Gym.

Week 7 brought the milling–which had been talked about. This took place in Maida Gym–where else!–and took the form roughly of a boxing match. I say roughly because clearly the Airborne organisers had never heard of somebody called the Marquis of Queensberry!

We were pitted against another Platoon and roughly paired off according to height and weight. Once in the ring we were obliged to slug it out toe to toe for two one minute rounds. This was to test our aggression–to see if we could dish it out and, just as importantly, to see if we could take it! The two contestants had to stand in their respective corners–one blue and one red–along with the PTI who acted as their second. When the time came for action, they had to stand to attention and call out their name, rank and number. This done a whistle shrilled and they charged out of their corners to clash like two rutting stags in the centre of the ring. Three officers seated at a table judged each brawl.

The other recruits had to sit on a gym bench waiting their turn to take part. In order to speed up things, the next two in each line were gloved up and ready to go. Some of the encounters did not last their allocated span. Whenever a fight was over the gloves were removed and put on to the next recruit so that they could be ready for action.

During the brawls in the ring, blood flowed freely from noses and mouths as one would expect. It was a bit disconcerting to be given a freshly used pair of gloves and find as you waited your turn that a rare blend of recruit blood would be seeping on to your bare knees.

When my turn came I climbed into the ring to be taken in hand by Grogan who was acting as my second. He checked that my gloves were securely tied and in a clear attempt to wind me up said "You've forgotten your f****ing handbag!"

I snapped to attention: "Private Grant–23525694–Sir". The whistle sounded and off I charged to clash violently with my opponent. In the first few exchanges I received a haymaker on the side of my head. My head felt as if it had exploded and put paid to my normal vision. I could barely focus and just kept punching blindly, hitting and being hit until the first round ended. During the interval as Grogan sloshed water on my face and hissed urgent instructions in my ear, I was more concerned that I still could not see properly.

The whistle sounded and round two exploded into action. I was glad that we did not require to show any ring mobility because if my opponent had been able to move around I doubt very much if I would have been able to locate him. My blind slogging went on remorselessly and I was aware of hitting the target, but equally aware that I was taking considerable punishment. Suddenly I was aware that I was punching empty air and a sense of panic struck me that I had lost contact with my opposite number. Then I was aware of Grogan wrapping his arms round me in the middle of the ring and his words "Stop it you mad Scots b*****d–he's down!" And sure enough, my opponent had finally gone down under my blind assault and the fight was over.

I was adjudged the winner. Standing in my corner as this was announced, still not able to focus properly, covered in sweat and with the salty taste of blood in my mouth, I certainly did not feel like a winner. Cpl Grogan seemed happy with the outcome and ruffled my hair in an affectionate sort of way as he stripped off my blood stained gloves.

The Milling cost 124 Platoon another casualty. It was an unspoken role that during the brawl in the ring that you never ever gave ground. One of our number Hargreaves from Norwich who was a superbly fit runner and was shaping up as a more than competent soldier was the next to go. He lacked aggression in the ring and retreated so much that despite warnings he back-pedalled his way out of 124 Platoon and out of the Parachute Regiment.

On the Friday of Week 7 the Confidence Course claimed another victim Joe Armitage from Manchester fell off a ramp and broke his wrist.

So we entered Week 8 now thirty six in number. We were now almost the senior Platoon on parade heading for the final week weeks of our training. By this time we fitted into the Depot scene like old soldiers. Our confidence in our hard won physical condition reflected in everything that we did.

The highlight of Week 8 was the Log Race. This had been much talked about throughout our training and was regarded as the supreme physical test. It was designed to be a severe test of fitness, stamina and the ability to work as team members under prolonged stress. The event was held in the area known as the tank tracks just outside Aldershot. The Platoon was divided roughly into four teams of nine members. Once out on the tank tracks we took possession of what seemed to us as a scaled down version of a telegraph pole. The team members tied their toggle ropes at different points over its length, so that with a combined effort we would lift it off the ground. We then had to race against the other logs over a course of about a mile. This course lay along the rough tank track ground, and then up what was known as Trig Point Hill, round the concrete trig point on top and then back along the course to finish were we had started from. Trig Point Hill was a steep incline of loose stones like a scree slope. The Log

Race turned out to be a minor social event in the Aldershot calendar as various people turned out to spectate. As we prepared for action, we felt a bit like gladiators in ancient Rome as they prepared to entertain a holiday crowd.

At last the four logs were lined up. A starting pistol cracked,and amid scattered cheers from the onlookers, the logs charged off towards Trig Point Hill. Running half doubled under the weight of the log was anything but easy as the log continually swayed wildly and made constant and painful contact with your leg. Trig Point Hill was reached after some effort and then the hard part kicked in as we had to drag the log as we slipped and slithered over the loose stones to reach the top. Reaching the top turned out to be the easy part! Going downhill, the log seemed to take on a life of its own and we had to fight, not only to keep our footing, but also restrain the log's downward plunge. Halfway down I was aware of the recruit behind me falling as he lost his footing and then cry out as he was dragged over the stones with his hand trapped in his toggle rope. Over my shoulder I saw Grogan and another PTI leap into action and with some difficulty cut the unfortunate recruit free and drag him to the side to avoid the other logs. I could not make out who it was, but took in the fact that his denims were ripped and that he was bleeding profusely from the face and hands.

We hit the bottom of the hill and got the log back onto an even keel. Grogan caught up with us. "Right–this log! You're now a man light, so Whittaker and Grant you'll have to stop f****ing coasting and give it some real effort!" We did our best to oblige him and got back as the second log home. We then had to run the couple of miles back to Maida and a more than welcome shower.

My final recollection is of being violently ill in the showers as the cold water hit me. It was the first time in my life I had been sick through pure physical effort.

The Log Race brought about three more empty bed spaces. Rick Skelton who had fallen on Trig Point Hill was now in the tender care of Cambridge Military Hospital, and two others who had come home on the last log were binned. They had been under observation for some time and their poor showing in the Log Race had simply confirmed matters.

So Week 9 saw 124 Platoon as the now senior Platoon and boasting of thirty three members.

Sgt Sharman expressed his surprise that his Platoon was still in a healthy condition and that so many of us were hanging in. The emphasis was now on the forthcoming Passing out Parade and so drill and even more drill was the order of the day.

The fitness side was not neglected and we were now doing ten laps of the Confidence Course on our daily visit. Cpl Grogan and his acolytes still punished us in the gym–putting a final end of course polish on us as they put it.

On August 30th Malaya, the last of Britain's major Asian colonies, became independent as 170 years of British rule came to an end. The world was changing and we wondered what implications it would have in the future for us as Britain's once proud Empire was dismembered.

On Tuesday 10th September I celebrated my twentieth birthday–if celebrate is the right word–with a cup of strong NAAFI tea and the knowledge that I was still on the course.

We were told that on the Friday we would be informed as to who had passed the course or had not. This was to allow the ones who had passed to concentrate in the final week for the passing out Parade on the next Friday 20th September.

A very nervy week ensued with everybody trying to work out if they had passed and meanwhile the pressure ground on relentlessly.

Friday 13th–what an appropriate date!–came round and we were asked to assemble in an empty billet block to await Sgt Sharman and his dreaded mill board. Sharman arrived flanked by the corporals and the PTI staff who had nursed us through the course.

His address was brief–simply telling us that he would read out certain names from his sheet. The names called out were to leave and return to our billet. The names not called out were those recruits who had not passed and they were to remain where they were as an officer would be coming to advise them on their options army wise.

Sharman commenced: "Armstrong" and Henry with a broad smile left the room. "Bateman–Davidson–Evans–Francis–Gamble–Haddon–Lancaster–Liles–"–and Wolf stalked off giving me the thumbs up on his way past. Sharman continued "Ward–Whiteside–Whittaker–Wood". I was left watching the ones who had been passed over and the look of sheer disappointment on their faces. In some cases many were blinking back tears. Meantime Maclean and I waited as our names as latecomers to the course were last on Sharman's list. We knew that he had finished the list of names proper and for a brief moment he lifted his head as if he had finished. I held my breath–surely not–and then almost as an aside Sharman said "Grant".

I was up and out of the room like a shot from a gun to join the others. "Christ!" said Wolf as I walked into the billet "I thought that they had rumbled you at last". "You must be joking" I replied and joined in the general jubilation. In all only fourteen of us had passed.

We were taken off to be congratulated by the Depot Commanding Officer Major Corbould. In a short talk to us he said: "Well done and welcome into the Parachute Regiment. I know that many of you are only here thanks to National Service–in a sense in opting for the three year engagement you can be classed as mercenary National Servicemen! Three years in my opinion is not long enough from this Regiment's point of view. We make a considerable investment in you. By the time we train you as soldiers and in parachuting and settling into one of the battalions we only have a relatively short time to get a return on our investment. I sincerely hope that some of you will make a long term career with Airborne Forces. You have proved yourselves fit to join this unique fighting force. I wish you the best of luck!".

By the time we had returned to the billet the other recruits had departed leaving us amidst a sea of empty bed spaces.

Week 10 was spent in getting everything ready for the Passing Out Parade. However, we had one more hurdle to pass. This involved an interview with a psychiatrist called the PSO (Personnel Selection Officer) and Cpl Meredith assured us that although we had passed Basic Training, a bad report from the PSO could still fail us.

We were, as a result, mildly apprehensive as we assembled in the ante room to the PSO's office. We had to go in one by one and as each recruit's interview was over, he left by another door so we had no idea what awaited us. When my turn came I entered the room to find an elderly Major seated at a desk covered with files. I saluted smartly and was asked to take a seat in a hard backed chair in the middle of the room. The Major proceeded to ask me all sorts of questions about my family background, how had I enjoyed basic training and why I had elected to serve in the Paras.

My answers were a bit guarded and defensive as I did not quite know what to expect. He indicated that the interview was over and relieved about this I saluted once more and headed for the exit door. As I did the Major suddenly fired a question at me "Grant–will you jump?" A strange request I thought, but maybe he wanted to test my reflexes. Nine weeks of following orders blindly kicked in. I turned towards the Major, put my feet together and executed a small leap in the air. As I landed with a clatter I saw a look of sheer disbelief on the Major's face. "No–no!" he said wearily "I meant will you parachute?" "Oh yes–Sir. Most definitely!" I responded and fled the room.

Friday 20th September came round–a lovely, crisp autumn day with sunshine dappling the tree lined square. The salute at our Passing Out Parade was taken by Air Chief Marshal Sir Dermot Boyle GCB, KCVO,

KBE, AFC and the Champion Recruit of 124 Platoon was adjudged to be 'Blackie' Gamble.

We marched off to the Maida parade square for the last time–a piece of Aldershot real estate that we had trampled over so much in the past weeks. Coffee and biscuits were set up for the after Parade gathering. We tucked in along with Sgt Sharman, the Corporals and the PTI staff along with some of the proud parents who had been invited. The Air Chief Marshal accompanied by Major Corbould circulated among the company making small talk.

Wolf's parents had turned up for the big day and 'Blackie' Gamble and I were standing with them over a cup of coffee. The Air Chief Marshal descended on us and, after being introduced to Mr and Mrs Liles, he congratulated Gamble, our Champion recruit. He asked Gamble if his parents too had come along. "Don't have any parents, Sir! I was raised in a Blackpool orphanage." The Air Marshal, slightly wrong footed then changed tack and asked him what he had done in civilian life before being called up for the Forces. "Well Sir, I had me barrow on the Golden Mile" supplied Gamble. The Air Marshal looked blank at this reply. Seeing this Wolf chipped in helpfully "What he means Sir–is that he was a spiv!" The Air Marshal moved on suitably enlightened.

When the post Parade party was over Sgt Sharman wished us all the best and informed us that early tomorrow we were off to the Parachute School at RAF Abingdon in Oxfordshire. We cleared out our lockers and packed our kit bags ready for the move. This done, we hit Aldershot town for a pub crawl to bring down the curtain on our basic training stint.

Saturday dawned and we were on our way by train chaperoned by Cpl M Meredith. En route we followed an old Para tradition and, with due ceremony, lobbed our red tabs out of the moving train window. I watched mine flutter away to land on the trackside and now it felt as if basic training was well and truly behind us. I returned to the carriage to join the others who were in full voice, led by Woody.

> "The train that I ride is twenty nine coaches long,
> Oh, the train that I ride is twenty nine coaches long,
> The train that I ride is twenty nine coaches long,
> I'm worried now–but I won't be worried long!"

This particular train was bound for disembarkation at Didcot station and then on to RAF Abingdon where the final step in our quest to become Paras would be enacted.

CHAPTER 6

No 1 PARACHUTE TRAINING SCHOOL R.A.F. ABINGDON

21st September–15th October 1957

"A Paratrooper is someone who hangs around
waiting for Opening Time!"
RAF Abingdon graffiti.

The fourteen members of 124 Platoon disembarked at Didcot station to be informed that there was no room for us at RAF Abingdon. Instead, we were to be billeted at a former Fleet Air Arm station at Culham some six miles away. Our Culham base turned out to be a collection of World War 2 vintage black Nissan huts set in a wooded area with a very basic dining hall and a small NAAFI unit to relax in.

We settled in and, as the next day was Sunday and our course did not start until Monday, we naturally looked forward to a relaxing day off after the rigours of basic training. It did not turn out that way. About 800 paratroopers from the 1st Battalion (1 Para) descended on Culham en route to take part in a major airborne exercise that entailed dropping in Denmark. They seemed to be everywhere in their camouflaged denison smocks while we, still wingless wonders, kept a low profile.

1 Para were due to fly out from Abingdon in the early hours of Monday morning. That night they slept round the wooded area wrapped up in ponchos and the thin Army blanket.

Little fires glowed with shadowy figures hunched round them. In the morning they had gone leaving only a trail of rubbish and blackened, smouldering fires. Naturally, we got the job of area cleaning after them!

After breakfast we were loaded into a three tonner truck to make the journey to Aldershot. As we drove out of Culham, the narrow road outside the camp was littered with abandoned cars and push bikes. A couple of harassed looking policemen were prowling among the vehicles with notebooks in hand. Some elements of 1 Para had gone into nearby Oxford to sample the night life and, on finding the late night public transport service wanting, had decided to liberate some vehicles to solve the problem.

RAF Abingdon soon came into view shrouded by early morning autumnal mists. Our first port of call was an introductory talk by the Station Commander. He welcomed us to RAF Abingdon and explained that our Course–No 452 Basic Course–would last some four weeks. The course would comprise two officers and fifty five other ranks. Apart from our Depot fourteen graduates, the others were from various detachments of the 16th Independent Parachute Brigade. The first eight days of the course would be devoted to ground training. We would then proceed to two parachute descents from a balloon car and then six from aircraft.

On the satisfactory completion of eight parachute descents we would be regarded as having qualified and be issued with our parachute wings. The course members were then divided into groups and allocated an instructor known to all as PJI (Parachute Jumping Instructor). Our instructor introduced himself as Sgt Starzaker, or as he said to give him his full name–Sgt 'Non-refusal' Starzaker!–whose proud boast was that he had never ever had a pupil that refused to jump.

He led us on a guided tour of the Station and in particular, the massive hangar where the ground training would take place. All the various pieces of training equipment were explained to us in some detail. In the afternoon a parachute was brought out and laid out on the ground while Sgt Starzaker pointed out its component parts. Looking at the parachute draped on the ground, it was difficult to grasp that in a week or so we would be entrusting our lives to one just like that. We were allowed to try on the chute, struggling into the body harness with the four straps that fitted into the central locking device on our chest.

Next day, ground training started in earnest. We spent days of rolling on mats with legs clamped together and shoulders suitably rounded in order to make the approved parachute landing roll that we would be expected to do on landing. This was gradually stepped up to increasing heights. We hung in parachute harness suspended from the hangar roof going over and over again the recommended mid air drill and emergency actions. Then it was outside to a device called the Tower and doing controlled descents from about eighty feet under Starzaker's watchful eye.

We used to lunch in the large RAF dining hall and some system blared out popular music continually. The Top Twenty song of the moment was Paul Anka's 'Diana' and it was played so often we were word perfect. Elvis Presley's 'All Shook up!' was running it as a close second.

Starzaker told us that 'All Shook Up!' was an appropriate song for the way that we would be feeling next week when parachuting began! Truthfully, by the end of the week we were bored stiff with all the repetitive ground training and were looking forward to the real thing. In September 1957 an outbreak of what was called Asian flu was sweeping the country. The normal death rate relating to ordinary flu had risen dramatically and the Ministry of Health was issuing daily statements. The sick bay at RAF Abingdon had started to take in its first victims and fingers were crossed that it would not interrupt our course.

Jumping proper started on Tuesday 2nd October. We were taken out to the airfield where a huge barrage balloon hung in the air with a balloon car suspended below it. This car was an open carriage with a doorway across which was a metal bar. The Balloon was tethered to the ground by means of steel hawser which was operated from the back of a truck.

Another RAF truck drew up and we were issued with our parachutes which we put on and had the general fitting checked. I was in the first quartet invited into the balloon car by a noisily cheerful Sgt Starzaker. As we entered, he fixed the strops issuing from our parachute pack to the strong point bar fitted into the roof of the car. the metal bar was placed over the doorway with a clanking sound.

"Right then!" he called out to the truck crew "Up 800 ft–four lovely lads jumping to die–no sorry!–dying to jump!"

With that we were off as the truck crew operated the winch and the balloon rose lazily into the air. There was a marker flag on the hawser at each 200 ft so Starzaker could look over the edge and work out our ascent progress. The wind whistled through the wires suspending the balloon car making a rather mournful sound.

"Who's going to tell a joke then?" said our instructor who seemed to be enjoying himself enormously. "You–Whittaker–you tell the first one." Ron licked his lips and started off on some joke but gradually it tailed off as he lost the thread of his story completely. Mind you, not that any of us were really listening to him!

"That's a helluva attempt at a bloody joke–What's wrong with you?–Got something on your mind?" was Starzaker's only comment.

By now we had reached the height for action. Starzaker removed the metal bar like a hangman testing the drop before an execution. He motioned me forward to stand in the door as first man out.

This was it. As I stood in the door bracing myself against the constantly moving motion of the car, I looked down at the airfield far below me where even the hangars looked like miniatures. Tucked discreetly behind one of the hangars was an ambulance. The red cross painted on the

roof was only too evident from my dizzy perch! I did not have long
to dwell on this as Starzaker slapped my shoulder and bellowed "GO!"
in my ear.

I went. I was aware of falling through space and my boots floating up
almost level with my face until the comforting jolt of my chute opening
checked my descent. I was floating free and looking up I saw the most
glorious sight of the white parachute canopy blossoming against the
backdrop of the blue sky. The descent was straightforward and in landing
I could see the other chutes in the air as the other occupants of the car
came floating in to join me. It was a great feeling to collect the chute and
stroll back to where the others were still apprehensively waiting their turn
to jump.

An RAF Officer with a megaphone was on hand to comment on a
jumper's performance in mid air if he was not carrying out his drill properly.

In the afternoon we turned up for our second balloon jump.

Starzaker was still in ebullient form. As the balloon ascended he
rounded on us "Seeing as how you are no bloody good at telling jokes–
how about singing a hymn?"

So we ascended with the strains of 'Abide with Me' floating down to the
course members on the ground. Starzaker said if this hymn was good
enough for the Titanic then it was good enough for his balloon car!

The second jump was a slight variation on the first. This took the form
of exiting through a circular hole in the middle of the floor of the balloon
car. On balance we all preferred leaving by the door rather than through
the floor as it made you more aware of leaving the balloon car.

By the end of the day we had all achieved the requisite two balloon
jumps. The following day was spent in talking about our balloon
experiences and brushing up on certain aspects of our mid-air drill.

We were supposed to have a flight in an aircraft on this day. This was a
recognised part of the course as most of the course members had never
flown before. For some reason no aircraft was available and so we were
denied this pleasure.

Thursday the 4th was our next day of action when we were due to do
descents from a Hastings onto the nearby dropping zone of Weston-on-
the-Green. We set off late morning and on board with us was the RAF
Station Commander dressed in a light blue jump suit with a flat type
parachute on his back. Two RAF despatchers were at the front of the
aircraft, securely tied to the strong pointwire that ran the length of the
aircraft. We sat in two lines on hard metal seating that ran along the two
sides. We were to exit from both doorways–the one on the left was the Port
side and the one on the right the Starboard.

The flight was relatively short and the two doors were swung open and down below us we could see the green English countryside.

The Station Commander standing near the open door suddenly wheeled and pointed dramatically at the rear of the plan. Our heads, Wimbledon like, all turned in that direction. We could see nothing amiss so we turned our heads to look again at the Station Commander–but he had gone!

When he had distracted our attention he had exited smartly out of the open door. It was just like witnessing a conjuring trick and certainly broke the ice for us.

In our turn we had to hook up our strops to the strong point wire and a despatcher came along making a final check on our equipment.

The red light above the doors glowed. "ACTION STATIONS!" came the cry. We stood in line swaying as the Hastings throttled back with our gaze on the red light–then it switched suddenly to green and the stick began to exit from the aircraft.

As I neared the door I could see the parachutes of those who had jumped opening, and the patchwork quilt of the countryside below.

I did not have long to take in the spectacle as, when I left the doorway, it seemed as if a giant hand had whisked me away as I was carried away on the slipstream. Soon I was floating free with the roar of the aircraft engines diminishing in the distance. A gusting wind made control of the chute a bit tricky and also for a harder than usual landing.

Once we had gathered up the collapsed chutes, it was back by truck to Abingdon through the dreaming spires of Oxford. Lunch in the dining hall and then we were off for a repeat performance over Weston, and we were half way through our jump programme.

Asian flu struck our group and no less than nine members of our course fell ill and had to report sick. Among the casualty list were three of 124 Platoon–Wolf Liles, 'Blackie' Gamble and Bob Ward. They would go on to complete their jumps at a later date, but this left eleven of the original Platoon still 'on course' in a manner of speaking.

On Saturday the 5th we woke to learn that on the previous day the Russians had inaugurated the space age launching a man-made satellite. This artificial moon known as Sputnik-1 was even now more than 500 miles above the Earth, taking 95 minutes to complete a circuit at 18,000 miles per hour. Russia had beaten the United States in the race to be first in space!

It was the next week before we tested the space above Weston again. We parachuted from a Hastings in the morning and in the afternoon from an ungainly shaped aircraft called the Blackburn Beverley.

The Hastings jump was interesting. When the green light glowed and we shuffled towards the door I found myself just behind Colin Bateman. As he approached the open door the aircraft suddenly lurched to the right which threw us both off balance. Instead of exiting forcefully, he hit the side of the door and then spun away in the slipstream. My forward impetus was even more affected and it caused me to hit the door frame painfully with my shoulder and then be plucked away by the slipstream. Instead of having the aircraft behind me as I jumped, I was now facing the wrong way and had a birds eye view of the aircraft doorway fast disappearing and a fleeting glimpse of the despatcher's anxious face. My spinning action in the slipstream had the effect of, when my parachute eventually opened, that severe twists had developed in the lift webs leading from my shoulders to the rigging lines. I had to spend some time kicking my way to unwind the twists before landing. On the deck was Sgt Starzaker who was less than complimentary.

"Grant–what are you and Bateman playing at? I have trained you to leave the aircraft door forcefully, haven't I? You two were standing in that bloody door like two Soho tarts waiting for business. Get a bloody grip–and I want to see a better performance this afternoon!" We did our best to oblige him.

Next day, Thursday, we prepared for our night time descent. We donned our parachutes and climbed into the waiting Hastings as darkness began to settle over RAF Abingdon. I ended up as No 2 on the starboard side as we flew over Oxford with its street lights winking far below us. Over Weston as we stood in the door, I was able to look over No 1's shoulder into the darkness outside, and down below watch the car headlights on the country roads moving like slow glow worms.

Exiting into the darkness was a new experience and it proved difficult to determine how the dropping zone lay below us. Another chute suddenly loomed up out the darkness and I extended my arms and legs as we had been told to do in training. I bounced off part of the canopy and rigging lines of the other chute. This brought an urgent shout of "Hey, f***k off up there!" from the intrepid skyman on the receiving end of my attention. A full moon hung in the sky which made the drop quite a spectacle when we were all strung out across the sky.

I seemed to come in backwards in landing and did a backward somersault which enmeshed me in my rigging lines and most certainly would not have met with Starzaker's approval. A bit stunned after this unorthodox landing, and as I gathered both my breath and collapsed chute, I was glad of the covering darkness.

Jump No 6 safely completed, we stopped off at a small country pub for a celebratory beer or two.

With only two more jumps to go, Abingdon seemed hell bent on wrapping things up by the end of the third week.

This was accomplished with two more jumps on the Friday and Saturday from the workhorse Hastings over Weston. This time the last two jumps were done with us equipped with weapon containers. In future all our descents would be with the weapon container, as in the battalions we would carry in them all the necessary weapons and equipment for our infantry role on the ground. The weapon container was designed like a huge canvas wallet. Into this would be packed our rifle or Bren gun, ammunition radio set, mortar bombs and any personal equipment.

The container was suspended from two D-rings on our parachute harness and also had a leg tie to secure it to our body. After we had exited and the parachute developed, the container had to be lowered away. This was done by first releasing the leg tie and flicking the quick release hooks attached to the D-rings. The container would plunge away from us and hang suspended by means of a 20 ft nylon rope firmly attached to our main harness. Starzaker assured us that if we ever landed still attached to our weapon container, not only would we not be able to carry out a parachute roll, but it would also spell the end of our rock and roll days!

On Saturday 12th October when we had safely landed and completed our eighth and final jump we gathered on the airfield. There, in a very informal ceremony, the Station Commander shook our hand and presented each of us with our coveted parachute wings. The Commander's indecent haste at our wings ceremony was due to the fact that he was down to play in a golf competition.

We were not too upset by this, as the fact that we have achieved entry into the airborne brotherhood was uppermost in our minds.

That night we celebrated in Oxford wearing uniforms bearing the newly sewn on parachute wings for all the world to see. It was a sobering thought that only eleven of us had seen the whole course through from the forty eight hopefuls who had assembled in Aldershot in mid July.

Our three Asian flu invalids in sick bay would, no doubt, complete their parachute course and join up with us at a later date.

But now it was time to head home for a well earned week's leave and look forward to battalion life that lay ahead of us.

CHAPTER 7

HOLDING AND DRAFTING COMPANY

October '57–January '58

"One crowded hour of glorious life
Is worth an age without a name".

Anon

Returning from leave in late October I found it hard to realise that it was a little over three months since I had first stepped off the train at Aldershot with little idea of what lay ahead of me. The agent's window still had the poster for "The Mousetrap" play and now had another sign stating that the play, after its 1,998th performance on 13th September, had now officially become Britain's longest running play. I wondered that now, having beaten the record, how much longer the play would last.

We had to report to Holding and Drafting company in a barrack block just down the lines from Maida. As I passed Maida I saw a recruit Platoon heading out for a road run with PTI's screaming at them and felt a sense of relief that all that was behind me. The 124 Platoon survivors gathered in our new billet and there was much talk about what battalion we would end up in, and also if we would all be posted together. Before this was decided, we had to go on a weapons cadre being introduced to all the weaponry that we might possibly encounter during battalion service.

In the middle of the second week 124 Platoon received notification that most of them were going to be posted to the 2nd Battalion (2 Para), but I was to be an exception.

Somebody, trawling through our records, discovered that I was in possession of a Scottish School Higher Leaving Certificate and I was to be considered for higher things! This took the form of being put down to attend an Infantry Clerk's Training Course in Chichester later that month. I protested that this was not my idea of why I had joined the Army, but to no avail.

Meantime the space race was well and truly on with Russia launching a second satellite containing a dog called Laika. This pioneering canine would supply valuable information on how animals respond to prolonged weightlessness so it could be a precursor to future manned space flights. All heady stuff.

On a more mundane level, I presented myself in late November at the Unit Clerk's Training Centre at Chichester. The Course that assembled was comprised of some forty soldiers drawn from every conceivable regiment in the British Army.

Two pleasant surprises came my way that November. Firstly like all 124 Platoon members, I discovered that we had a pay rise! Due to the fact that we were now qualified parachute soldiers, we received an extra £2 two shillings a week giving us a weekly income of £7 twelve shillings. Riches indeed!

The other surprise was unexpected promotion!

Three members of our Clerk's course were temporarily promoted to acting unpaid Lance Corporals for the duration of the course. The other two recipients were two Scots Guardsmen and the basis for this promotion was that we had done longer, and more intensive, training than the general run of recruits.

I could not resist sending a postcard home to brother Gerry who had seen out his two years in the Camerons quite happily as a private. The postcard read "3 months in this Man's Army–and I am a Lance-jack! How about that then?"

His reply postcard put things sort of in perspective as it read "A Lance Corporal!–so what, so was Hitler–and look what happened to him!".

As Course Corporals, our main task was to take turns in marching the Course on early morning parade for inspection by the Officer Commanding the unit.

We would march the course down to the square, check the dressing, and then stand them at ease. We would remain out front facing the course members waiting for the arrival of the officer. Eventually we would hear his approaching footsteps crunching on the gravel before coming to a halt. At this point we would bring the Course to attention, about turn, march up to the officer and salute informing him in ringing tones "Course 452–all present and ready for your Inspection, Sir!"

The officer would return the salute, and conduct a perfunctory inspection before dismissing us. Our last task was to march the Course away to commence the day's studies.

The Course, we were informed, would last some four weeks and in it we would be taught not only how to type, but all the rudiments of office management.

I, for my part, could not wait to get through the next few weeks and get back to rejoin my fellow 124 Platoon graduates in 2 Para.

We were allowed to go out of the camp each evening in uniform reporting to the Guardroom on leaving and departing. Curfew was at 11 p.m. prompt.

Sometime in the second week, we got word that Humphrey Lyttleton and his Jazz Band were appearing at a dance in nearby Bognor Regis. Four of us decided that we would take in this dance, but first we had to circumvent the Guardroom routine.

We did this by cutting a section of the wire fencing round the camp so that we could slip in and out without putting the Guardroom to any bother.

On the night we slipped out like a prison of war camp break out and caught a bus to Bognor. Our quartet consisted of one of my fellow lance-jacks and fellow Scot 'Jock' Young, 'Taffy' Evans from some Welsh regiment and Ian Bentley from REME. The dance was most enjoyable until Taffy, who was in his own opinion, a 'ladies man' started to dance in an over amorous fashion with a local girl. Her fiancé, naturally, took exception to this and an altercation took place in the foyer area.

We were in the bar when word came to us that Taffy was in some trouble. When we arrived on the scene we found Taffy and the fiancé locked in combat with a couple of bow tied doormen trying to restore order. Jock Young and I immediately dived in to help take Taffy out of the affray. This turned out to be a big mistake. Other doormen, on seeing more uniformed bodies getting involved, rushed to help out and things sort of escalated. As I caught hold of Taffy's arm to pull him away, I was dimly aware of a doorman rushing in at my side. Next thing I knew I received a full blooded punch to the side of my face that sent me crashing to the floor. This initial assault was followed up by the doorman delivering several forceful kicks to my prone body. I curled up and shielded my face as best I could so as to avoid more facial damage, whilst executing one or two parachute rolls to take me clear of the action.

By this time both Jock Young and Taffy had got clear and legged it from the building leaving me to the wrath of the doormen. As I scrambled to my feet, I took all this in and decided in the circumstances that a speedy and tactical withdrawal was called for. I ran out of the main door and chased down the street to catch up with the other three who were all virtually unscathed.

The side of my face felt like I had been kicked by a mule.

We clubbed together to get a taxi back to Chichester.

As we drove out of Bognor with me still nursing my sore face I was reminded of something I had read about Bognor and its royal connection.

It happened when King George V was on his death bed in the royal residence in Bognor Regis. Sunk in his final coma with all his grieving family and medical attendants gathered round him, he rallied for a moment and asked where he was. A doctor leaned over and said "You are in Bognor, your Majesty".

"Bugger Bognor!" exclaimed the stricken King and, falling back, he breathed his last. Leaving Bognor that night, I had a certain fellow feeling with our late monarch.

Back at Chichester, we slipped through the wire and back to the billet. In order not to disturb the rest of the sleeping billet, we crept to beds without putting the lights on. Next morning I awoke with the side of my face still sore, but otherwise I felt fine. On the way, whistling to the washroom I got the first inkling that things were not as good as they seemed. Another course member, returning from his ablutions, nearly dropped his washing gear when he saw me.

"Hey, what the hell happened to you?"

I made no reply but dashed to the wash hand basin mirror and reared back horrified at the apparition that stared back at me. I had received a small but deep cut to the corner of my eyebrow which had bled and the dried blood encrusted my face. For good measure my eye was blackened and the side of my face bruised and swollen.

Once the encrusted blood had been washed off, it did not look so bad, but there was little that I could do with my black eye.

Dressed ready for parade, I was assured that with my red beret pulled well down it sort of shadowed the discoloured optic. To make my day complete, it was my turn to take the Course on parade.

I marched them down to the square, stood them at ease and waited for the Inspecting Officer. It was a frosty, early December morning and to my dismay I felt the cut on my eyebrow start to leak blood again and slowly trickle down my cheek. There was nothing I could do about it as I heard the officer's footsteps behind me.

I called the Course to attention in as confident and normal a tone as I could muster, about turned and marched up to the officer to deliver my state of the course address. In the watery sunshine flooding the square I was acutely aware that in no way did my beret obscure my facial damage, now highlighted by the rivulet of fresh blood coursing down my cheek.

The Inspecting Officer looked suitably aghast and took some time to compose himself before stating "Corporal–dismiss this parade–and report immediately to my office!" before stalking off.

When I attended his office he was incandescent with rage. He, naturally, thought that I had been fighting with another Course member, and all that this would mean for the unit morale. I made a clean breast of things without grassing on my errant companions who had also been on our night out in Bognor. I got the feeling that he was somewhat relieved at my full explanation, but nonetheless he demoted me and awarded my stripe to another more deserving Course member. In addition, I had to report to the Guardroom every night at 9 p.m. and 11 p.m. until the end of the course.

I had to return to the billet to unstitch the lone chevron from my uniform. I decided not to bother sending another post card to Gerry on this occasion.

A Lance Corporal for just over a week–I wondered idly if I had not set some kind of record.

I rejoined the class and made the decision to lie low, complete the course and get back to Aldershot and life with 2 Para.

On our last week on the course we were delighted to learn that National Service respected nobody. The Memphis Draft Board in the United States had called on Elvis Presley–'The King of Rock and Roll' for his two year stint in the armed services.

Elvis's reported comment to the world press on learning of this was "I think it will be a great experience for me". We would all second that!

The course broke up on Christmas Eve and, like the others, I was adjudged to have passed "Standard Trade Test for Clerk–Group 'B'–Class III" whatever that was supposed to mean. I spent a frugal Christmas Day in the camp and watched the Queen's first televised address to the nation before proceeding on leave on Boxing Day.

I got back to Inverness in good time to celebrate New Year in traditional fashion. On Hogmanay there was dancing in the Caledonian Hotel Ballroom to Harry Shore and his Ballroom Orchestra–admission 7/6d. Otherwise you could pass the night at the Northern Meeting Rooms with local band Jimmy Wilson and the Melotones featuring Eck Wilson as vocalist–admission 4/-with the first 100 dancers allowed in free!

So it was goodbye to 1957–and welcome to 1958 and whatever it might hold.

CHAPTER 8

WELCOME TO 1 PARA!

January 1958–June 1958

"Fill the unforgiving minute with 60 seconds worth of distance run"
Kipling

Early in 1958 I reported back to Holding and Drafting Company to get my kit organised and get ready for the move to join the others in 2 Para. To my surprise, I was told that I was joining up with 1 Para so, with packed kit bag, I made my way down the road to Albuhera Barracks home of the 1st Battalion. Reporting as usual to the Guardroom I met up with the redoubtable figure of the Provost Sergeant 'Nobby' Arnold. Nobby, a former boxer with a badly reset nose, did not make for the most gracious of welcoming committees.

Directed to the Orderly Room, I met with Chief Clerk Bob Bryant who informed me that I would be employed as a clerk in his Orderly Room and as a member of HQ Company. I tried to explain that I had been put on the Clerk's course against my wishes and stated my preference of joining a rifle company. Bob Bryant patiently explained that as the Army had gone to the expense and bother of teaching me a trade, then I had to make use of same. He did say that once a replacement clerk hove into sight, my posting to a rifle company would be given due consideration. Until then I had to be satisfied with that. A bed space in HQ Company billet was my next port of call and I was issued with a red lanyard and flashes to denote that I was now in 1 Para.

It was relatively easy settling into life in the Orderly Room and I soon got to know my fellow members of HQ Company.

My bed was next to a slim, fair haired chap called Goldsack.

Over a cup of NAAFI tea he filled me in with all I needed to know about life in 1 Para. I disclosed to him that I was only in the Orderly Room on a temporary basis as the Chief Clerk had promised me a move to a Rifle company. Goldie raised his eyes at this information. "If old Bob makes you a promise well don't hold your breath! However, if you do get a move just make sure it's not to bloody 'C' Company!" "Why not?" I

59

enquired intrigued. "Oh" went on Goldie "You want to avoid that shower at all costs. In another age they would all have been shipped off to the Colonies and good riddance to them. Always in trouble that lot. Mind you, in the last year they got two former champion recruits from Depot– Cpls Brown and Hunt–in an attempt to improve the quality a bit. Do you know that last year they actually mutinied against an officer!" "A mutiny!" I echoed "That sounds like serious stuff." "You're bloody right it was!" continued Goldie. "But it was all kind of hushed up in the end. It involved an American Exchange Officer–a Major Gartain–some highly decorated Korean War hero–who was temporary O.C. of 'C' Company. Well, 'C' Company felt he was going over the top a bit with them, so one night they refused to turn out on some punishment parade and instead a lot of them went boozing down town. On strike they said they were–only the Army have a different name for it! There was hell to pay, but it was all hushed up to a great extent in case the Press ever got wind of it.". Goldie sipped his tea and now that he had caught my attention, went on to enlarge on things,

"To show you what they are like–there was this female called Myrna. She was going with some bloke in 'C' Company until he got demobbed. By this time Myrna was obsessed with all things military and used to haunt the Havelock Arms where 'C' Company hang out. She must have been a raging nymphomaniac or a touch simple, because she used to bestow her favours on any 'C' Company Tom who glanced in her direction. They used to smuggle her into the billet at weekends and she would move from bed to bed like a bloody mobile hot water bottle. So, needless to say, she ends up with one up the spout! Even in her advanced pregnant state she would sail into the Havelock like a ship in full sail and it was a real laugh to see 'C' Company personnel down their pints and scarper. Nobody could say with any degree of certainty who the actual father was–not even Myrna. When the baby was born–it was a boy–Guess what? That's right–she called it Charles! Somebody even put a sign on their noticeboard saying 'To 'C' Company and Myrna–a son Charles born 12th February 1957".

Goldie then drank heavily on his Naafi brew allowing me time to take on board the outrageous and not to say immoral conduct of 'C' Company. He lowered his mug and got back into full flow.

"Back in Cyprus in 1956–you'll never believe what they did! The Commanding Officer at that time for some reason best known to himself started to tighten the screw on the Battalion. Now this in turn began to have a serious effect on 'C' Company's way of life. So–you know what they did? They bloody well set fire to the C.O.'s tent!" Goldie must have seen the shocked look on my face and he hastened to reassure me. "Oh the C.O. himself was OK–happened to be feeding his face in the Mess when his residence was torched. Of course nobody was ever caught for it–no names–no pack drill as they say–but it bore all the hall marks of a 'C' Company action.

It was their way of passing a not so subtle message to the C.O. to lay off and start behaving like a C.O. is expected to do. He duly obliged and battalion life returned to as normal as life in 1 Para can ever be.

Bloody shower so they are–breeding ground for the f/*ing Mafia if you ask me!"

His now empty mug was slammed on the table as he delivered his final verdict.

"No, take my advice Jock–and steer clear of that lot!"

I thanked Goldie for this invaluable advice, and mentally stored it away for future reference.

Meanwhile the space race was hotting up with some obscure Senator from Texas called Lyndon Johnson making calls for the USA to overtake Russia. The USSR faltered in its progress when Sputnik-1 disintegrated as it entered the earth's atmosphere.

In late January violent anti British riots broke out in Cyprus. The hitherto peaceful minority community of Turks had taken to the streets despite a curfew, burning Police cars and stoning Security forces resulting in 100 Turks injured and 2 killed. It was eventually halted after an appeal by the Turkish leader Rauf Denktash while the Governor Sir Hugh Foot was returning in haste to the troubled island from a meeting of the Baghdad Pact.

Word soon spread that our Chief Clerk had taken a £20 bet with the Adjutant that 1 Para would be in Cyprus before the year was out.

I settled into life in 1 Para combined with my duties in the Orderly Room. Life still involved road runs, days on the range, guard duty and parades, as we were not allowed to forget that first and foremost we were airborne soldiers.

At the end of January, we were notified that HQ Company was to take part in an exercise in Southampton. HQ Company members were to be spread around among the Platoons that were to be picked from among the rifle companies. L/Cpl Bill Browlie and I were allocated to a Platoon from 'C' Company and Goldie's only comment to me was "F***k your luck!"

The Southampton exercise was a fairly big combined civil and military affair. An H-bomb was supposed to have been dropped on the city and the exercise was to see how the various rescue elements could handle things.

The Paras were to be rushed from Aldershot to see how quickly we could be on the scene. Dropped off the trucks at various key points, our task was to patrol into the city centre to prevent looting and suchlike by some of its more enterprising citizens. We departed Aldershot at 2 a.m. from the battalion square in a succession of three ton trucks. It was freezing in the backs of the slow moving convoy, and when we were finally dropped off on the city outskirts we were all stiff and cold. Dawn was breaking as we set off through the deserted streets in small groups of four or five soldiers. I found myself in the company of four 'C' Company stalwarts, and one called Duffy turned out to be a fellow Scot from Aberdeen.

After a while we left the residential housing area behind and found ourselves in a more commercial part as we neared the city centre. We stopped at a shop with a sign that read "Confectioner" and one of our group stepped into the doorway. The entrance door to the locked shop was set slightly back from the main display window frontage with a narrow side window.

"Here!–Jock, cover me!" said the soldier in the doorway.

He had picked up a sodden discarded evening newspaper from the gutter. It was draped over the muzzle of his rifle and, with one quick movement, he slapped it hard against the side window so that the paper adhered to the glass. I moved in as requested to shield him, more than a bit puzzled as to what he was up to. Over my shoulder I saw him raise his rifle and slam the butt forcibly onto the paper plastered to the window. There was a dull crump and the window shattered noiselessly. Another blow with the rifle butt, and a sizeable hole opened up in the window with shards of broken glass falling silently into the shop or sticking to the sodden newspaper. He knelt down and, reaching in, started to haul out as much as he could within his reach. Once he had filled the pockets of his denison smock he passed other items over to me and I stuffed my share of the booty into my pockets. I was astonished at the slickness of the operation and it must have showed on my face. My fellow shop breaker laughed at this and said "Just a spot of pillaging–we will give rape the gobye–seeing as its a Sunday!" We shared out the pillaged goods with the others before proceeding on our way. Munching on a liberated Mars bar, Goldie's words of advice came back to me–here I was a temporary member of 'C' Company for a matter of a few hours and already I was party to a breaking and entry.

Once we reached Southampton city centre our role, for what it was worth, was over and we had to hang about for hours before being transported back to Aldershot. Now that I had settled into life at Albuhera Barracks, I was determined to put one ambition to rights and that was to see a major football match. Back home, I had been so involved in my own sporting activities I had never even seen a Highland league match, while basic training and Abingdon had left no opportunity to do anything else.

On 1st February I headed up to London with the sole intent of taking in my first real major game of football.

I bought a newspaper to check the sports fixtures and instead my attention was caught by the front page article. America had finally followed Russia into space by launching a 30 pound satellite called Explorer into orbit. An earlier attempt at launching a satellite last December had failed when it blew up on the launch site. The sports fixtures was my immediate concern. I knew by heart most of the major London teams like Arsenal, Spurs, Chelsea and Fulham but I had no idea where they were based in the city. The fixture list showed me that Arsenal were at home to none other than Manchester United. The Busby Babes– what a mouth watering match!

A tube station map showed me quite clearly how to get there so, after a pub lunch, I made my way to Highbury stadium. Once there I stood open mouthed at the imposing frontage of the stadium as it was far grander than anything I had imagined.

I crushed into the ground with 60,000 other spectators and stood on the crowded terracing facing the main stand. The game kicked off at 3 p.m. and the action was pulsating with the huge crowd thrilling to the spectacle. The highlight for me was a goal scored in the first half by the United wing half prodigy Duncan Edwards. He scored from all of thirty yards with a bullet like ground shot that I don't believe Kelsey in the Arsenal goal even saw. For my part, I had never seen a football struck so hard. Arsenal contested that match with spirit and their centre-forward David Herd notched up a hat-trick. United ran out winners with a 4–5 score line with further goals from Taylor (2), Charlton and Violett. The youthful, fair haired Bobby Charlton, I noted from the match programme, was the same age as me.

Later that day I headed for Chessington to spend the rest of the weekend with Wolf at his parents' house. I was more than satisfied with my first major football match under my belt.

Thursday 6th February saw me on guard duty at Albuhera Barracks.

Guard duty came round on a rota basis and involved eight soldiers parading at the Guardroom at 10 p.m. There they would be inspected by the Duty Officer and then the Guard would be posted.

Four men would be posted to patrol round the perimeter of the camp armed with pick axe handles for a two hour stint known as a 'stag'. Guard duty meant that you would be doing two separate stags and trying to catch up on sleep as best you could in between.

I came in from my second stag at 4 a.m. chilled and looking forward to
a cup of tea before trying to grab a couple of hours sleep before reveille
proper sounded.

At this time in the morning, most people would be either out on
guard, or crashed out on the bunk beds at the rear. This morning nobody
was sleeping.

They were all hunched round a crackling radio set. "What's up?" we
asked. One of the group at the radio lifted his head. "It's Man. U.–their
plane crashed in Germany–they're all killed!" We stood in shocked
surprise. At that time details were very sketchy and we were left without
much further news. That morning, as the Battalion stirred into life, the sad
news became only too apparent. It was as if the Battalion had suffered a
close family bereavement as gradually news of the scale of the disaster was
released. Of the team that I had thrilled to along with the Highbury
crowd only a few days previously, no less than seven members had
perished–Roger Byrne, Tommy Taylor, David Pegg, Bill Whelan, Eddie
Colman, Mark Jones and Geoff Bent. Matt Busby, the manager, was in
hospital seriously ill and had received the Last Rites. Duncan Edwards
too, was fighting for his life in the Munich Recht der Isaar Hospital. The
entire nation was in mourning it seemed, but football like life had to carry
on. Thirteen days later United had to fulfil a 5th round FA Cup tie
against Sheffield Wednesday. Some new replacement players were
bought, and Wednesday were swept away on a tide of emotion as United
won 3–0.

Two days later another body blow hit the stricken club as the seemingly
indomitable Duncan Edwards died as a result of his injuries. By this time
Matt Busby was off the danger list, and was able to tape record a message
for the United faithful in time for their match on March 9th against West
Bromich Albion. It was reported that fans wept openly as his recorded
hospital bedside message echoed across a packed and silently grieving
Old Trafford.

On a somewhat happier note Bobby Charlton, although hospitalised,
had recovered and was back training with the team. He was back in the
side by April, scoring against Sunderland. The United team were carried
on this public wave of emotion to the FA Cup Final on May 3rd against
Bolton Wanderers. They lost the final 2–0 and so ended the most tragic
season in the club's history.

March 24th saw the long awaited day when Elvis Presley turned up at
the Draft Board Headquarters in Tennessee to commence his National
Service. The 23 year old singing sensation turned up accompanied by his
parents and manager 'Colonel' Tom Parker. Pictures of the Rock and Roll

King getting his short back and sides haircut were flashed around the world. His teenage fans were said to be devastated at the thought of losing their idol until 1960.

Life in Aldershot had settled into a routine, lightened only by occasional weekends in Chessington with Wolf at his parents' house, which for me had become a real home from home. Intensive field training became the order of the day as unsettled reports from both Cyprus and the Middle East continued to filter through to us.

In June 8th riots in Cyprus resulted in four deaths and seventy people hurt, while in mid June Britain stated that it would send in paratroops to Jordan to back up King Hussein's security forces. Our Chief Clerk was delighted that his bet now seemed to be a sure thing!

June 20th saw the exiled Archbishop Makarios, leader of the Greek-Cypriot community reject a British peace plan and once again Cyprus was put under an island wide curfew.

On the football front, a brilliant Brazil team defeated their Swedish hosts 5–2 in the World Cup Final in Stockholm. Starring for the South American team was their unstoppable winger Garrincha and the 17 year old scoring prodigy called Pele.

On my personal front, despite repeated requests Bob Bryant had not honoured his promise to release me from my Orderly Room duties.

One weekend in late June, Wolf and I sat long over our espresso coffees in the Kenya Coffee House and reviewed our future prospects. There was no guarantee that we would ever get abroad, and as we were regarded as National Servicemen, promotion or anything else would also have a very low priority. We resolved to take action and put in applications to join the Special Air Service in order to change the tempo of our short lived military careers. It was widely known that SAS members were for ever flitting in and out of the country to exotic foreign climes. What better way to break our present stalemate!

We were both due to proceed in the next week on summer block leave so we decided on our return to slap in the applications for the SAS. Meantime, Wolf suggested that we did not tell his parents about the proposed move until it was fait accompli.

We shook hands on it and the next week I headed home to Inverness for my leave period. Little did we suspect that events would occur in the next few days that would change our plans dramatically.

CHAPTER 9

RED DEVILS
FOR THE MIDDLE EAST!

July 1958

"One does not go to Hell to light a cigarette!"
Greek Cypriot proverb.

I came off the overnight express at Inverness and headed immediately for the station buffet. As I tucked into my morning roll and coffee, I became aware of another diner who was reading a newspaper, casting glances in my direction. He lowered his paper and addressed me. "You a deserter, then?!"

I thought at first it was his attempt at humour until he pointed to the stark headlines in his paper. "RED DEVILS FOR THE MIDDLE EAST!" What marvellous timing–no sooner do I go on leave than the balloon goes up.

The Middle East had indeed flared up into a sudden and dangerous crisis with the bloody overthrow of the Iraqi monarchy. A group of young Army officers inspired by Colonel Nasser of Egypt delivered a coup against the pro-Western regime of King Feisal of Iraq. The twenty three year old King was murdered, along with his Crown Prince and Prime Minister. This coup exerted pressure on both Jordan and Lebanon and the west was forced to intervene. American marines waded ashore at Beirut in a show of strength while Britain's Transport Command delivered some 2,000 paratroops to Amman in Jordan to bolster up King Hussein.

I reached home, and that evening the local Police Sergeant delivered a telegram to the effect that I had to return to Aldershot soonest.

Arriving back in Aldershot from my brief leave I walked up the same route as I had taken almost a year ago. There, to remind me, in the ticket agency window was the poster for "The Mousetrap"–now in its sixth great year and still going strong.

Aldershot had a slightly unreal air about it as the three parachute battalions had flown out over the past two days.

66

At Albuhera Barracks I found myself on a rear party with about thirty or forty others who had missed out on the main airlift. We spent a week or so tidying up the deserted Barracks after the battalion's hasty departure.

Our rear party finally took off for Cyprus flying by Comet, and it was quite a personal highlight for me, as it was the first time I had actually landed in an aircraft.

We exited from the Comet into the baking heat of the mid-day sun at Nicosia airport and my first steps on foreign soil! A couple of three tonner trucks collected us and drove through the city until we reached the place where 1 Para were based. The Middle East may have been in turmoil, but Cyprus itself was not exactly a haven of peace as 31 people had been killed in the last week as EOKA continued with their struggle.

We were delivered to Camp Whittington, a large tented area enclosed by a barbed wire fence close to the British Military Cemetry.

The Camp itself sat on an escarpment overlooking the city, with tents drawn up in neat and orderly Company lines.

Everybody we met was sun tanned and we, pale skinned new arrivals, were the butt of much good natured humour as we stood out like sore thumbs. I reported to Bob Bryant at the Orderly Room–or should I say Tent!–and he had good and bad news for me. The good news was that he was going to honour his promise and post me to a rifle company, but the bad news was that it was going to be 'C' Company!

I shouldered my kit bag and went through the lines until I had located 'C' Company. In the first instance, I reported to CSM (Company Sergeant-major) Fred Graham who indicated a tent that I could take up residence in. The tents held five soldiers and things were pretty basic with sleeping bags on the sand. 'C' Company were out on a route march so I had time to settle in before my fellow campers arrived back.

The four members of my tent were Paddy Tomkins, an Irishman now living in Manchester, Dave Bushell from Essex, Tony Surtees from Workington and Jim Steel from London. Introductions were quickly made and I was filled in with all I needed to know about 'C' Company.

I enquired as to what the CSM was like. "Oh, Gog?–He's not the worst!" supplied Paddy Tomkins. I was intrigued. "Why do you call him Gog?" It turned out that at some stage the CSM had worked as a Sergeant in the MT (Motor Transport) section. At one and the same time, a cartoon in one of the daily tabloids had an ancient Briton called Gog who was responsible for maintaining the Roman chariots! Hence the name.

Next morning, I was formally welcomed to the Company by our Officer Commanding Captain Tony Grant (no relation). He duly informed me that I would be replacing the current company clerk Cpl Rice who was due for demob. I realised then that Bob Bryant had been a bit devious when he had granted me my posting request. Geordie Rice took me under his wing and proceeded to show me the ropes. I confessed to him my disappointment at having been duped into being clerk in a rifle company.

"Don't be bloody stupid!" said Geordie "This is one of the best numbers going. Properly handled you hold a certain amount of unofficial power– you see you act as a buffer between the Sergeant Major and the rest of the Company. Mind you, you have to step carefully. There's a thin line between the boys regarding you as a grass or being a genuine and dependable filter of information. You will have the senior NCO's treating you like an equal as they try to ferret out information. You handle it properly and life can be very enjoyable pal!"

I decided to take his words to heart and make the best of it. My duties were minimal, just keeping some simple records like the individual Parachute Descent files and typing out the daily Company Orders.

When that was done, I was regarded as an ordinary rifleman with Company H.Q. so I reckoned that I now had the best of both worlds.

Life in 'C' Company started with a bang literally. We were leaving Camp in a convoy of trucks to take part in amphibious assaults with part of the Mediterranean Fleet. A truck carrying 8 Platoon capsized on its side as the road verge gave way. This happened, ominously enough, just outside the gates to the military cemetery but although the soldiers were shaken nobody was seriously hurt. We, in the trucks behind had no idea of what had happened and suspecting either a mining or an ambush we baled out into the ditches at either side of the road with weapons bristling. Word soon filtered back and we were able to resume our journey.

We embarked on two ships "Anzio" and "Reggio" and spent most of that day and night in hitting the beaches from small assault craft. On our return trip to Nicosia in the early hours of the morning the Greek residents of the village Ayios Andronikas had set fire to some Turkish houses. We were not allowed to stop or get involved, but it was a reminder to us of continued troubles in this island.

The other two Parachute Battalions were in the meantime in Jordan lending moral support to the beleaguered King Hussein. It fell to us to provide the manpower at Nicosia airport for their airlift of supplies. Supplies like rolls of barbed wire, oil drums, ammunition, food rations and crates of all kinds had to be loaded onto a shuttle service of Beverley and American C119 aircraft. It was hot, dusty work and we toiled away like ancient Egyptian slaves dressed only in PT shorts and boots. We worked through the night in the clammy heat as the loaded aircraft flew off into the night for Amman, and empty return aircraft came in to land. If we had to wait to load an aircraft, we simply cat napped at the side of the runway. During one such lull two 'C' Company members went into look at the cockpit of an American C119 that was being refuelled. Under the co-pilot's seat they found a long greenish box rather like a large sardine can. It had a pull ring on it and when this was operated the lid peeled back to reveal a veritable cornucopia of good things. It was the aircraft's emergency rations! The contents revealed delights like Camel and Chesterfield cigarettes, chewing gum, cookies, chocolate bars and other equally tempting items. Word soon spread and 'C' Company set about the task of liberating as much of the goodies as possible. The lids could be tucked back in such a way that only a very close inspection could tell if it had been tampered with.

Incoming C119's soon became an irresistible target.

'C' Company lines in Camp Whittington soon became awash with this stolen booty as successive airport shifts returned from their duties. The items were considered too hot to be stored in the tents along with one's personal gear, so people started to dig holes in the sand close to their tents to bury their personal haul. They would work out how many steps from a certain guy rope stanchion, dig a hole to bury their goods and then mark it with a large stone.

Other finer details were not ignored either. Camel and Chesterfield cigarettes were housed in everyday Players and Woodbine packets and the incriminating original packets were confined to the murky depths of the Deep Trench Latrines (Toilets).

'C' Company prided themselves in being very professional in everything that they did! One night as an airport shift returned, one soldier called Perkins went to bury his haul. Dog tired, he quickly dug a hole to bury it before heading to his bed for some sleep before reveille sounded. He made the mistake in the darkness of digging his hole outside the wrong tent, and in the morning could not remember for the life of him what tent it was.

This came to my attention when Gog stalked into the Company office tent and declared that in his opinion Perkins had a touch of sun stroke. He had come across him digging holes around a tent. When he had challenged him, Perkins had just mumbled something or other, shouldered his trenching tool and ambled away.

That same night Gog had gone to the Company Office tent to finish some report and then decided to head for the Sgts.' Mess for a beer before retiring. To his amazement he heard the sound of digging, and on checking saw Perkins in the darkness still busily engaged in digging holes like a gopher that had gone into over-drive.

Gog knowing the reputation of 'C' Company was desperate to know what it was all about. In the morning he rounded on me in the office.

"There's something going on Grant–what do you know about it?!" Mindful of Geordie Rice's advice to me, I stepped warily. I volunteered the information that there was currently a competition on the go among the lads to see who could dig the fastest slit trench, and perhaps young Perkins was getting some practise in. Gog looked unconvinced at this explanation.

The airport duties was hard grinding work on top of our normal day's routine and seemed as if there would be no end to it. One night a kindly senior RAF type took pity on us and invited us into their NAAFI so that we could relax over a beer during our break. A special concession was made of our dress code, and so about twenty of us invaded the NAAFI and mingled there with the off duty RAF servicemen.

At first all went well as we relaxed and slaked our thirsts. I noticed at one point three of our lads sitting drinking and chatting to some RAF chaps. After a while a heated argument started to develop and one of our lot, Jim Bromilow, started to raise his voice and indulge in finger pointing. Paddy Tomkins also spotted this, and observed "We had better watch out–looks like Bromilow's coming to the boil!"

With that I saw Bromilow suddenly down his pint glass and swallow dive across the table to head butt the RAF chap full in the face. He went down in a welter of blood, the table and chairs were knocked over and it seemed as if all hell broke loose. It became like a Wild West saloon with men battling, glasses flying and bodies running for cover. In no time 'C' Company personnel found themselves all alone in the midst of a ransacked NAAFI. The same kindly RAF Sergeant who had extended the invitation to us was hastily summoned and we were ordered back to Camp Whittington forthwith.

On the way back in the somewhat subdued truck, Chris Newton said to the still smouldering Bromilow "Hey Jimbo–what the f***k was all that about anyway?" Jim was only too keen to put forward his explanation. "That fat bastard was slagging off Bolton Wanderers, so he was!" "But Jim, you're not even a bloody football fan–so what are you on about?" "Well–it's the bloody principle of the thing" maintained a still indignant Bromilow. You had to laugh.

The outcome was that everybody was banned from using the airport NAAFI facilities for good. At one and the same time the aircrew had discovered their pillaged emergency rations and there was hell to pay. A snap inspection of 'C' Company lines by RAF Police revealed little, but nobody was in any doubt who had been responsible. Perkins had given up his fruitless nocturnal digging of the company lines as it slowly dawned on him that somebody else had chanced on his secret cache. It was just as well, as Gog was about to take steps to have him certified!

About this time the airlift of supplies to the troops in Jordan was deemed to be complete and our airport duties ceased.

Word then filtered down to us that we were to be prepared for an impending operation to relieve the AF Station Habanayah in Iraq which was under threat.

Training took on a new and urgent intensity. The principal training area was in the Mesaoria, the flat, arid plain outside Nicosia. This plain, lying between the Kyrenia Range in the north and the Troodos Mountains in the south whose Greek name defines 'Between the mountains' was known to us as the dreaded Dustbowl. Here we would train in the height of the noon day sun when the heat shimmered off the stony and sandy soil. We were told that this was to get us used to the temperatures that we could be facing in Iraq. The two water bottles that we carried on the back of our equipment belt was our only means of slaking our thirst. By midday the water was so tepid that all it lacked was a tea bag to make a more than passable cup of tea!

We were issued with a daily supply of salt tablets to help replace the bodily salt that we lost running around doing endless section attacks. One day before we set off for the Dustbowl, Captain Grant had the bright idea of dissolving the tablets in our water bottles, as by his reckoning, this would have the same end result. I did not think this was sound advice and refrained from so doing. The wisdom in doing this was borne out later that morning when the Platoon stopped for a smoke and a drink of water and everybody started gagging as they attempted to drink the warm sea-like water in their bottles. Our OC's character was vilified in a rich variety of oaths.

One day as we sat after a hard session in the baking heat, somebody remarked idly "Wonder how Elvis is making out?" There is little doubt a hard session in the Dustbowl would have given the Rock and Roll idol a different perspective on life!

Later every afternoon we would jog back the few miles to the Camp for a welcome shower. Our sweat soaked clothes had to be washed immediately because if they dried out, the dried bodily salt would make them as stiff as a board.

Goshi range to the south also became part of our training agenda especially for live firing exercises. The sand at Goshi was of a white powdery variety that seemed to reflect the heat. Standing around in our rubber soled jumping boots could become a minor torture and the reflected glare of the white sand made for a migraine type headache. One day on Goshi I was involved in firing a 3" mortar with one Scouse Jim Bailey who bore more than a passing resemblance to the actor Harry Belafonte. We were unhappily based in a slit trench directing mortar fire on a particular objective, when along came our Commanding Officer Lt Col Reinhold with Gog in tow. The CO stood there with binoculars to his eyes and started to criticise the angle of elevation of our mortar. The bombs were not falling quite to his liking. Several times he sharply asked us to alter our sighting until Scouse Jim finally snapped, "Why not fire the f****r yourself?" was his suggestion to the CO. Reinhold just looked at him very coolly for a moment, "Put that man on a charge Sergeant Major!" he responded before moving off to inspect another part of our fighting machine. We knew that things were hotting up in another sense at the sight of a fleet of Beverleys and Hastings aircraft all lined up at Nicosia airport. Unofficial word came that we were on a 6-hour standby.

That night we lay on our beds in our tent contemplating an early morning departure into we knew not what. Paddy Tomkins told the story of a pal of his who served in 3 Para at the time of the Suez landing in 1956. As the aircraft in which he was in was nearing El Gamil airport, he was seated No 2 in the port stick next to a senior officer. Just before the sticks were stood to 'Action Stations' the senior officer turned to Kelly and said "Isn't it bloody great–today we jump into history!" Kelly's reply above the roar of the aircraft engines was less than historic. "F***k history! I didn't even like the subject in school!"

That night we slept fitfully waiting for the call, but in the morning word went round that the operation was off. A sense of disappointment swept 1 Para as we realised that all our training was for nothing. The only consolation was that our visits to both the Dustbowl and Goshi were at an end for the time being anyway.

I had settled well into life with 'C' Company and getting to know the rich variety of characters that made up the three Platoons.

Our CSM Gog ruled the company with a rod of iron. He was tall and slimly built with a permanently tanned leathery face of one who had spent a long time in the great outdoors in foreign climes. Rumour had it that he was utterly devoid of a sense of humour, but to be fair running 'C' Company did not give him much to smile about.

One afternoon after we had been stood down, a game of football was organised on the sandy parade square. Two of the corporals were selecting the teams and as I waited I flicked the ball on to my knee, then my head and cushioned it on my instep on the way down. I was aware of one of the corporals watching my party piece. He bore down on me. "Hey you– you've played a bit–where do you come from?", this query in a broad Scots accent. "Inverness" I replied. "Christ–why don't you speak like a bloody Jock then!" was his comment. I tried to explain that it was a well established fact that Inverness and Dublin were reckoned to speak the best

Queen's English without a trace of an accent. George Brown, with the ball at his feet, dismissed this, retorting "Aw–Belt up" Who asked you for your bloody life story anyway?" And so I was introduced to Cpl George Brown–a former Champion Recruit and now a leading light in 'C' Company. George Brown I soon learned was a forthright character who believed in calling a spade–a bloody spade!

Needless to say, my flash of footballing skill meant that I ended up on his team. With things more relaxed we were now allowed to go out into Nicosia, as long as we were armed and in parties of not less than four. This was fine for a time until drinking got out of hand and brawls broke out on a regular basis among troops of various units. Dave Bushell and Paddy Tomkins came back one afternoon somewhat shaken. They had been sitting in some bar enjoying a beer with a couple of others when some drunken passing soldier decided to spray the bar with automatic fire which put a sharp end to their afternoon's relaxation.

The entire company was on parade one morning as two bruised and battered American servicemen toured our assembled ranks, trying in vain to identify their assailants of the day before. This event, along with increased EOKA activity, reduced our down town afternoon outings as it was felt that having drunken Paras wandering around fully armed was not a very bright idea.

About this time, the authorities tried to get a grip on the excessive drinking by bored servicemen. A special poster was produced that showed a typical British Tom seated at a tavern table. His hair tousled and his battle dress top undone, the Tom was clearly in a drunken stupor with the table littered with half finished drinks. The stark caption below the poster read 'DANGER–EXCESS DRINKING CAN KILL!' Nobby Arnold the Provost Sergeant proudly displayed this on his Guardroom wall until some 1 Para wit defaced it by writing below the caption 'A PARA IS NOT AFRAID TO DIE!'

We were in a strange kind of limbo at this time. We had been stood down from the proposed Iraqi operation and, with the other two battalions preparing to pull out of Jordan, word began to circulate that we might be going home.

Gog decided to fill in the time with having 'C' Company spend their days on patrol exercises which was a nice military term for walking tours. After breakfast Gog would lead Company HQ out of the Camp and we would strike out across the Mesaoria towards the distant Kyrenia range. When we reached the foothills we would scale the jagged Kyrenia peaks, and once on top the view was panoramic and breath-taking. Far down below us were the fertile orange and lemon groves running down almost to the sea shore.

In the very far distance across the blue Mediterranean one could just make out the faint purplish haze of the Anatolian Mountains of mainland Turkey.

We clambered down to the fertile green coastal strip to the sea where we would spend a couple of hours swimming and lazing about before heading back over the peaks to camp. One day we stumbled on Newman's farm full of scrawny Jersey cattle that had a milk bar and proved to be a welcome refreshment stop.

Each day Gog would vary the part of the range that we would tackle. We visited St Hilarion, a mediaeval castle and fortress that sat on a high peak overlooking the town of Kyrenia. This ancient pile reflected the architecture that spanned some ten centuries with Byzantine, Frankish and Venetian influences. Another day we struck further west and descended the steep hillside into a village called Bellapais. We entered the village in single file while the villagers looked on silently. In the middle of the village, a group of men were drinking coffee under the shade of a large bushy tree. Gog told us that this tree was called the Tree of Idleness and that Bellapais citizens had the reputation of being the laziest people in Cyprus.

Nearby was a magnificent ruined Abbey–the 12 century Abbaye de la Paix–the Gothic Abbey of Peace. We obtained entry to the Abbey and although most of it was in ruins, part of it was still used as the active village church. Inside the Abbey, out of the scorching heat, it was a haven of shaded coolness. Walking over the large stone flagged floor we admired the colourful icons and other religious trappings. The sense of peace and tranquillity was very real.

We left Bellapais to scale the rugged outcrop and mouldering turrets of Buffavento. This castle is one of the three great Crusader castles built to guard Northern Cyprus against the Saracens in the Middle Ages. Halfway up the mountain I looked back on Bellapais, with its serene Abbey dozing as if transfixed in some medieval dream. How we enjoyed those superb days climbing in Kyrenia with all its points of interest and the relaxing swimming sessions in the sea. It was all very welcome after Goshi and the Dustbowl.

On our return to camp after a shower and evening meal we would get a can of beer and head, as often as not, for the open air cinema. This was built on a sloping part of the hillside with rows of sandbags set out as seating. We would sit there clad only in our PT shorts, can of Keo beer in hand, watching the latest release. When an aircraft took off from Nicosia airport it flew directly overhead, so that for a few minutes the sound track was blotted out. As an audience we were very well behaved, but at any time when a female appeared on the screen there would be a cacophony of wolf whistles and associated sounds. One night an old and disfigured crone appeared in a scene, and a lone member of the audience stood up wolf whistling, to our general merriment.

By this time our tent occupants had bonded into a fairly tight unit. They were all different–Dave Bushell a burly figure with a crew cut, Tony Surtees a tall rangy laid back individual from Cumbria, Jim Steel from London and Paddy Tomkins. Paddy was without doubt the most enthusiastic soldier I have ever seen–he even moaned with enthusiasm! This lithe, dark haired Irishman never seemed to stop talking and there was never a dull moment when he was about. He was, in addition, a considerable middle distance runner and his two great friends Denis Purton and Brian Hodgson used to talk tactics in our tent. When we went for a road run they brought a competitive edge into it to see who would be back first. On my first road run with 'C' Company I decided to tag along with them. It was a big mistake as this trio set off with a killer pace and soon left the rest of us behind. That was bad enough, but to get back to camp sweat stained and exhausted to find Paddy already showered asleep on his bed in a midday siesta was dispiriting to say the least.

Paddy was engaged to his fiancée Maree who lived in Manchester. His writing of love letters was a nightly event that drove the rest of us to distraction.

If a romantic film had been shown it seemed to inspire him, and he would toil late into the night composing his letter by the light of a guttering candle. The worst part was when he would wake me up to discuss the literary merit of some purple passage he had just written. In the end, although I had never met her, I felt that I knew Maree personally. In the end, a well aimed lobbed boot would be thrown at his candle and we could all get some sleep to face the day ahead.

One night as we lay on our beds we got to talking about the different reasons why we had joined the Army and the Paras in particular. Of course, Paddy just had to have the most colourful account. It appeared that with work scarce in Ireland, many young men came across to England to seek employment. Paddy came across with about six others and they found work labouring for British Rail on the tracks and lived in digs in Hitchin in Hertfordshire. After some months they would receive a letter calling them up for National Service. This was the signal to head back to old Ireland, wait for a spell until the dust had settled and then return to pick up their jobs again. Paddy had been to a film one evening and In the Pathe News he saw supplies being dropped by parachute for our ground troops operating in the Malayan jungle. When his letter came for National Service he went along more out of curiosity than anything else. When he saw the poster for the Parachute Regiment, he naturally assumed that this was the unit that fed supplies to ground troops from the air. When he also realised that the wage of £7 all found was better than his British Rail wage, he did not hesitate and signed on the dotted line. He took some convincing when he reached Airborne Forces Depot that, far from lobbing supplies to ground troops, that it was he himself who was to be lobbed out! We laughed ourselves to sleep that night.

One morning Gog gave me Company orders to type and now that the Jordan flap was over he had secured an old Dakota so that 'C' Company could take part in a Company drop next day. As I typed out the Flight Manifest lists it dawned on me that this would be my first battalion jump. However, in the morning we were due to parade for synthetic training. In this training we would use a mock aircraft to rehearse our aircraft drill prior to the jump proper. It was so long since I had qualified at Abingdon that I knew I was badly in need of this training.

Next morning as we paraded to go on synthetic training, myself and Bill Duffy who had arrived with me on rear party, were taken off to catch up on some Yellow Fever jabs that we had missed out on. As a result, we did not get any synthetic training. In the afternoon we attended Nicosia airport and drew out our chutes from an RAF van. The day for me had started badly and was now about to get no better. The chute that I had been issued with was a tangle of buckles and webbing. One of the shoulder buckles was rusted and seemed to be clamped to the webbing, and no matter what force I used neither buckle would move. Everybody else seemed to have slipped on their chutes with remarkable ease and were sitting around smoking. Not wanting to show that I had any problems, I put on my chute. The shoulder buckles that should have sat on top of my shoulders were anything but. One was situated somewhere over my left breast, and the other one somewhere in the region of my right shoulder blade. The rest of the webbing hung loose–I realised that I was really in no fit condition to take to the air, but I was too embarrassed to draw anybody's attention to the fact. We were jumping in shirt sleeve order due to the fierce heat and how I missed the comforting bulk of my airborne denison smock. We boarded the Dakota and took off. Our dropping zone was to be just outside a village on the Mesaoria on the way to Famagusta so the doors were left open for the duration of the flight. I drew some comfort from the fact that we still had to be checked by the air despatcher before 'Action Stations' and I was confident that he would see my predicament. The despatcher started to his task and when he came to me he just punched my quick release box to see that it was secure and then, to my horror, carried on down the stick.

The last thing we had to do was secure our parachute strops to the strong point wire in the aircraft. This was done by means of a clip hook secured by a thin wire clip. When I got my clip I saw to my increasing concern that it was heavily rusted too! I secured the strop with no great conviction and by now, despite the stifling heat inside the Dakota, I was breaking out in a cold sweat. We stood up on the red light and in no time the green glowed and with an almighty surge the stick took to the air. In a battalion jump, the closer the stick is in the air, then the closer they are once they hit the deck. This can be quite important if there are forces on the ground taking exception to your presence as a unit can get organised and into action more effectively.

I was aware of exiting from the Dakota into the bright sunlight, being shipped away in the slipstream, and then that magic moment as the chute blossoms arresting your fall. It will remain an eternal mystery to me how I remained in my parachute harness with loose webbing flopping all over my body, or so it seemed.

The landing itself was text book as we dropped onto corn stubble on an unfenced farming area just outside the Greek village. I lay there for a few seconds with the corn stubble pressing into my back, with above me the azure canopy of the sky with small fleecy clouds drifting. Life seemed very sweet at that moment as relief flooded through my entire body. Quite a number of the villagers had ventured out to watch the airborne spectacle. We were responsible for collecting our own chutes and taking them back to a collection spot. Two members of the port stick had collided in mid air and as a result had to take evasive action to miss the outskirts of the village. On landing they had got together to compare notes and have a quick cigarette. When Whitton went back to retrieve his chute, he discovered that some enterprising onlookers had filched it away. He was more than put out as he had his pay stopped until the cost of the missing equipment had been made good. Whitton was ragged for a long time that he was responsible for the women folk in the village sporting the nattiest line in lingerie in Cyprus.

As we returned to Camp Whittington that evening, word was rife that instead of returning to the U.K. with the other battalions, that we were to go on into action against EOKA. Well, maybe into action is a bit heavy, but from now on we were to be involved in Internal Security on the island.

CHAPTER 10

CYPRUS
DEATH IN THE
AFTERNOON

August 1958–October 1958

"There is no borrowing a sword in time of war"

Greek Cypriot proverb.

In early August we were at last informed that we would not be going home like the other two battalions at present in Jordan, but would be remaining in the island to become involved in Internal Security duties. Up to this point we had been too involved in our own intensive training to really take much notice of what was happening around us.

From time to time we would hear the dull crump of an explosion in Nicosia and afterwards a small mushroom like cloud would be left hanging in the hot, windless air. One Sunday was particularly active with no less than seven such clouds marking explosions in different parts of the city.

We were also introduced to the delights of guarding the Governor General, Sir Hugh Foot, at his official residence. His residence was a small estate on the outskirts of Nicosia looking towards the distant Kyrenia range. The house, naturally, was well guarded with a permanent presence of Military Police at the main gate. Our task was to patrol the fairly extensive grounds securely fenced and topped off with barbed wire. Although it was strictly against the rules to smoke on guard duty, we became very adept at smuggling in cigarettes and matches. They would be wrapped in cigarette foil and pinned inside our red berets so that we could enjoy a quiet smoke as we patrolled in darkness the wooded grounds. I used to always volunteer for the 4 a.m.–6 a.m. stag. I found it a strangely moving experience looking out from the security fence across the open plain to the distant bulk of the Kyrenia range. As dawn slowly broke over the small villages that studded the foothills of the range, the sounds of them stirring into the life of another day could be quite clearly heard. The strident crowing of a cock would be answered from another village and dogs barking as shepherds prepared to move out with their flocks. There is a certain magic as the cold night air leads to that delicious coolness, that only too soon gives way to the unremitting heat and glaring sun of another day.

Life in Camp Whittington was still fairly basic. The nearest thing to a NAAFI we had was provided by some enterprising Pakistanis. They had received permission to set up a tent and from there they dispensed tea and a special delicacy called an "egg sanny'. This was simply a hard fried egg slapped between two slices of bread. Basic it may have been, but nonetheless very welcoming and they did brisk trade. They called everybody 'mucker' and took our teasing in good part. We would tell them that they had no right to be attached to a Parachute battalion as they had never qualified as paratroopers! To this they would respond in their highly individual sing-song like voices "We nebber see the jump, mucker"!

A company rest camp was set up on the Kyrenia coast and various platoons would go there on a two day rota basis to relax. This break was much looked forward to by all members of 1 Para and helped relieve the boredom of camp life. We may have simply exchanged one camp for another, but this one looked out onto the blue Mediterranean as it lapped the shore. We lazed about swimming and sunbathing without a care in the world. One night we were even allowed to go into the town of Kyrenia to enjoy a drink in the small bars round the harbour. Unfortunately, drinking by some of our brethren got out of hand and a bar was wrecked. Military Police were called in and we were sent back to our rest camp in disgrace and Kyrenia was placed out of bounds. So, Kyrenia was added to 'C' Company's undistinguished battle honours!

In late August we did a battalion drop at Morphou in the west of the island. This time I made sure I was issued with an acceptable chute!

We flew in Hastings and Beverleys out over the Turkish coastline before heading back for Cyprus. I was No 3 in the starboard stick with Gog standing in the door, the red light reflecting on his helmet. Over his shoulder I could see the cornflower blue of the sea laced with white ripples. The light was still at red and I thought to myself, I hope the pilot had no plans to decant us early. Gog turned his head towards us and mouthed the words "Land Ahoy!" above the roar of the engines, and sure enough down below us we could see the rich brown soil coming into view as we passed over the coastline.

The green light flashed and we were off–the slipstream whisking us forcibly away until the entire stick was strung out across the sky. Other aircraft continued to shed their human cargo and the sky was suddenly full of chutes swinging weapon containers and assorted shouts as mid air collisions took place. The perfect windless conditions gave one plenty of time to look around and take in the stirring spectacle of nine hundred paratroopers descending onto the sandy wastes of Morphou. We spent the day perfecting some section and company attacks before being trucked back to camp.

On 7th September word came that the EOKA leader Colonel Grivas had called off the truce declared a month or so ago. We got our first experience of patrolling a couple of villages in the Kyrenia area to supervise an imposed curfew. Twice we observed an all night watch on a village suspected of harbouring EOKA gunmen.

Wednesday 10th September saw my coming of age and any self respecting 21st birthday should be duly celebrated. We did just that–about twenty of us crowded into our tent armed with an assortment of drinks, such as Commandaria wine, Keo beer, ouzo and sundry cans of NAAFI brown ale– not forgetting a bottle of whisky of dubious origin. As dawn came up, I was draped over the guy rope outside our tent with severe alcoholic poisoning. The reveille bugle sounded calling the sleeping battalion to another day, and I almost wished fervently it had been the Last Post for me!

Anyway that morning's seven mile road run in full pack sweated the poison out of my system in no uncertain fashion.

The next day Paddy Tomkins, Steel and Surtees returned from overnight guard duty at the Governor's house in a high state of excitement. They claimed to have seen the Governor's daughter, or some other nubile female house guest, getting ready for bed at an open window in a state of complete undress. It was a very warm, clammy night and it appeared she was doing some ballet like movements, quite unaware of the open window. Word spread quickly among the patrolling Paras and soon they had gathered under the cover of an olive tree to take in the erotic window display. On their return to camp next day, word spread even quicker among 'C' Company and guard duty no longer became a chore to be avoided. In fact Gog got quite concerned when he noticed that men, when told that they were on guard duty, were slapping each other on the back with broad smiles all round. Gog tried to find out what I knew. I tried to reassure him that going on Guard duty for the Governor was regarded as an honour by most of 'C' Company. Gog's comment on my explanation was unprintable.

However, the Military Police on permanent duty at the house must have got wind of it, because all window screens were drawn from then on.

We still managed the occasional slog over to Kyrena with lunch break at Newman's farm followed by our swim, but somehow we sensed the good times were coming to an end.

On 21st September a 1 Para champ was blown up by an electrically detonated mine and the driver Johnson had his leg blown off. The next night Surtees, on camp guard duty, was fired on from a moving vehicle and returned fire.

Paddy Tomkins was promoted to Lance Corporal about this time and we celebrated by going on yet another Governor's guard duty. On arrival we spoke with the Military Police at the main entrance before we were posted. Two of them were just leaving by jeep to go into Nicosia and not long after they left us they ran into an ambush. One of the redcaps L/Cpl Bell was killed. His funeral took place some days later in the military cemetery and we paused as the volley of shots rang out and the poignant strains of the Last Post sounded. EOKA were certainly stepping up their activities and on 26th September the British Army Chief General Kendrew narrowly escaped an assassination attempt.

The next day a truck from our 'A' Company was blown up and both Simpson and Elms wounded. Elms in particular suffered severe facial injuries and the loss of an eye.

On Wednesday 1st October 'C' Company moved to Famagusta to carry out road blocks and patrolling in that area in the face of increased EOKA activity. A British civilian was shot outside a chemist's shop in Larnaca–masked men shot dead a suspected Greek Cypriot informer, and four bombing attacks on army lorries resulted in two wounded. Friday 3rd October saw us playing an afternoon game of football when the game was abruptly stopped. Something had happened in down town Famagusta and our presence was required soonest. We kitted up, drawing weapons and ammunition before roaring off in the back of three tonner trucks towards the city. As we neared Famagusta the high walls surrounding the old city were black with people crowded up there shouting and waving us on. "They're Turks" observed Gog "And for some reason they are asking us to get stuck in!" As the trucks skirted the crowded walls before we entered the old city we felt a bit like Roman gladiators of old.

We were in radio contact, and orders came to drop off groups of troops at certain points. This we did and we were the last to get out at Hermes Street–Gog, Paddy Tomkins, Dave Bushell, Surtees, Steel and myself. Down the street we could see a small group of people gathered round a freshly laid patch of sawdust. Gog went off on a walk to find out some answers and soon returned grim faced. Two British women had been gunned down in broad daylight. A Mrs Cutliffe, wife of a serving soldier, and her daughter had been shopping for clothes for the daughter's forthcoming wedding when a gunman came up on them through the crowd and shot them in the back. Mrs Cutliffe was fatally injured, but the daughter had survived though badly injured.

Our immediate task was to stop and search all vehicles, demanding to see passes. We were thus employed in the early evening when Gog returned from checking on other company road blocks. He watched silently as we pulled a private car into the side and conversed politely with the occupants while we checked passes. As the car drove off Gog exploded. "What the f**k do you lot think you are on about, then? You look as if you are checking passes to a f***ing royal garden party! Watch me! Don't ever speak to the bastards–that's what bloody rattles them!"

With that a small van drew up with two Cypriots in it and the back of the open pick up was loaded with lemons. The driver stuck his head out of the window calling out a cheery greeting to Gog who was striding menacingly towards the van. Without a word Gog rammed his Stirling sub machine gun into the side of the van door, then grabbed the driver by his shirt front and started to drag him out through the window. The driver hastily undid the van door and fell out onto the roadside. Gog kicked him back onto his feet and pushed him against a wall. He made him lean facing the wall and kicked his feet out so that he ended up propped against the wall with his hands above his head supporting him. Gog now finally spoke as he turned to me and said "Frisk him". I frisked the trembling driver who had now been accompanied by his equally terrified mate. Passes were found to be in order, but still Gog had not finished.

"Search the f***ing van" was his next barked command. This involved the entire load of lemons being dumped on the road. "It's clean!" reported Paddy. The men were shoved back into their van and shot off with a squealing of tyres leaving us with a roadway awash with deserted lemons. "And that" said Gog "Is how I want to see a f***ing road block operating. Never ever speak to the murdering bastards–that'll teach them to shoot our womenfolk!"

The next vehicle pulled in was a saloon car with four male occupants. Gog stood aside as we moved into action. I rammed my Stirling into the side of the car leaving a dent that brought a quiet smile of approval from Gog. On the other side Paddy had his weapon almost stuck up the passenger's nose and the car was vacated quickly. Paddy and Steel kicked the men wordlessly against the wall in approved fashion, while Surtees and I commenced frisking operations. I had almost finished when Surtees tapped me on the shoulder and showed me the pass he had just been given. It was a Press pass belonging to a Daily Express reporter. In fact they were all reporters heading for a nearby Press office to wire their stories back to their respective editors!

Similar harsh treatment was meted out to all others who came into our orbit that night. It was most certainly not a night for any law abiding Cypriot to be abroad in. The frustration of the troops, that night was well and truly vented on any luckless Cypriot that crossed their path. At one stage we got hold of a radio and Dean Martin crooned "Volare" in the background as we manned our road block and continued with our roughing-up tactics.

Later in the night, Paddy and Tony Surtees were pulled off to patrol further afield leaving the three of us to continue to deal with passing vehicles and their occupants. Some buses had been torched, and Paddy managed to drag out one drunken driver who was fast asleep in the cab of his blazing bus. They returned before dawn, begrimed but happy. By this time the pangs of hunger were becoming evident after our all night stint and we knew from past experience that our breakfast arrangements would not be a priority. Our problem was solved when we pulled over a baker's van doing deliveries and liberated his produce in best 'C' Company style. This had to satisfy us until the early afternoon when we were stood down and trucked back to camp.

It had been a rough old night that brought little credit on the various troop units that cracked down on Famagusta that night. The fact that it resulted in deaths of four people and that the local hospital was fully extended in dealing with literally scores of injured citizens speaks for itself.

The EOKA gunman's cowardly action could never hope to justify the lack of restraint shown by our military crack down that night on unarmed civilians.

We returned next day to Camp Whittington and normal duties.

On Monday 6th October, Gog passed me a rather strange entry to be included in next day's Company Orders. It asked for volunteers for a "Q-Ship Operation" and stated that there was an element of personal danger attached to it–hence the request for volunteers. Naturally 'C' Company volunteered to a man! Everybody quizzed me as to what it was all about, but Gog had been strangely tight lipped about the matter. Some thought it might be cruising round the island in a yacht, checking on potential gun running from mainland Greece. Gog was swamped with applications, and seemed unsure how to go about whittling numbers down and, at the same time, maintaining a degree of secrecy. My suggestion that he pick the necessary volunteers from Company HQ members fell on fertile soil. The Company were duly informed that the operation would not now go ahead, while Gog selected six of us to attend a briefing. So it was Paddy Tomkins, Surtees, Steel, Bushell, Denis Purton and myself who filed into the briefing tent.

The "Q–Ship" title was explained to us. During World War 1 a Q-ship was used to tempt a German U-boat to the surface. Anti-submarine vessels were disguised as unarmed freighters or trawlers for this purpose. The U-boat would surface in order to destroy this soft target, only to find that the vessel would suddenly bristle with hidden armaments and start blasting them out of the water. This idea was to be the basis for our immediate operation. An RAF radar station was situated in a remote place towards the west of Kyrenia range. As a manned unit, it was supplied twice a week with mail and rations by means of an RAF truck.

En route this truck had to pass through two Cypriot villages. One in particular–we were never told its name–was openly hostile and had a reputation of assisting the EOKA gunmen who operated in the Kyrenia Range. Several times bombs had been lobbed at the RAF truck as it passed through on its way to the radar station. The latest had badly injured the driver and his armed escort. It was decided that enough was enough and that the time had come to strike back–hence the "Q-ship Operation"!

One of our Army trucks was painted with RAF roundels and the driver and escort would wear RAF uniform tops to complete the deception.

We six volunteers would be lying in the bottom of this truck fully armed, but out of sight. The truck would make the usual ration run, but only this time had the ability to strike back with some effect. To this end we sand bagged the bottom and sides of the truck so as to afford some protection against any exploding device.

We trained out in the Mesaoria for a couple of hours to get the drill right. We were to lie three on each side of the truck–one at the front, one in the middle and one at the rear. Our personal responsibility was the immediate arc to our front so that, no matter from what side the bomber struck, it would be covered. During training the truck would slam to a halt as if bombed and we would leap over the side of the truck, throw a stone to simulate a hand grenade, lie flat so as to avoid the blast, and then charge outwards with Stirlings at the ready. We did this over and over again until it was felt that we were all fully conversant with the drill.

On the morning of 8th October we were told all was ready. We drew ammunition and grenades from the armoury and set off in our newly commissioned RAF truck. Stan Wardlaw from the MT section was to be our driver. As we reached the outskirts of Nicosia the truck slowed down and a burly individual in civilian clothing clambered aboard. He had a strong Irish accent, and under his jacket a holster housing a type of pistol that we had never seen before. We were never told who he was or what his function would be. He sat beside me at the front, and in his only conversation said that he would strike the truck roof with his hand in the

Lovat Scout Boer War Monument –
that so impressed the author at a
tender age!

Beauly village square with the Lovat
Scouts Monument as it is today.

Beauly village square and monument
– circa 1915.

ALDERSHOT 1957

THE PARACHUTE REG.T

1ST BN.

HUGH - RECRUIT COMPANY

Joining 1 Para January 1958.

The raw recruit! 1st week in Recruit Company – 124 platoon July 1957.

Celebrating passing Recruit Company. The author and Arthur 'Wolf' Liles – September 1957.

Two fellow recruits Henry Armstrong and John 'Woody' Wood the 'Newcastle Brown' men!

Col. G. HEWETSON DSO OBE
COMMANDANT, AIRBORNE FORCES DEPOT

requests the pleasure of the company of

Mr Grant & Family

at the Passing-Out Parade of No. 124 PLATOON, RECRUIT COMPANY,

at which the salute will be taken by

Air Chief Marshal Sir Dermot Boyle GCB KCVO KBE AFC

at 10 15 AM on Friday 20 Sept 57 will be taking part.

in which PTE GRANT

Light Refreshments will be served after the Parade.

R.S.V.P. to O.C. Recruit Company,
Airborne Forces Depot,
Maida Barracks,
Aldershot, Hants.

124 Platoon.
Passing out Parade invitation.

4

Cpl. George Brown (extreme right) and posse! – on patrol somewhere in the Kyrenia range in Cyprus, September 1958.

The author at coffee break time in a "Hide"
in the Troodos mountains, Cyprus.
Operation 'Mare's Nest'.

The author and Denis Purton with
Sgt. Joe Murray (behind).
Golden Sands Beach – Famagusta recovering
from 'near drowning' incident.

INVERNESS MAN KILLED IN CYPRUS

Ambushed while Serving with Marines

An Inverness Marine has been killed in an ambush in Cyprus. Information was received yesterday by Mrs Macdougall, Police Buildings, Inverness, that her only son, Alastair, had been killed. He was 20 years of age and was a regular in the Royal Marines. He was formerly employed as a mechanic with Messrs Macrae and Dick, Inverness.

Alastair was on his second tour of duty in Cyprus. He was home on leave in the summertime and was to be demobilised in January.

Special anti-ambush training was being given to British troops in Cyprus yesterday after EOKA terrorists had claimed their 126th British victim—ambushed and shot in a lonely mountain road.

Paddy Tomkins – Troodos mountains for 'Sky-Man' read "Ski-Man!"

Alfie Holland and author (right) guarding an EOKA
'hide' in Kyrenia – Range Operation "Filter Tip"

Paddy Tomkins – Camp Whittington,
Nicosia – 'C' company lines.
"Who's for a 10- mile run, then?"

Paddy Tomkins on patrol in Upper
Lapithos, Cyprus.

Spanish air tragedy August 1959.

PARIS - NOTRE DAME 1959

Author on Notre Dame bridge. Paris in August 1959

Doreen Wright on same bridge in August 1959.

Start of Billy Butlin's John O' Groats to Landsend walk – March 1960 'Tex' Banwell and CSM Butler.

The terrible twins David 'Mitch' Mitchell and Jim Hunt. All at sea on the Sogne Fjord – Norway – Norway 1959. Exercise 'Bar Frost'

The author's final parachute descent being gratefully acknowledged. May 1960.

The author presenting the photograph of Doreen taken on the bridge at Notre Dame to her 87 year old widowed mother Mrs Abigail Wright (seated) and her aunt Mrs Ellen Steel, September 2000.

event of the bomb being thrown outwith the driver's vision. This made good sense to us.

We crouched down in the sand-bagged bottom of the truck as we neared the target village. Stan slowed the truck down and we lay on our sides looking upwards at the roof tops waiting expectantly for a black device to come sailing over in our direction! The normal sounds of village life filtered through to us–people calling to each other, dogs barking and children at play laughing. Children!–I suddenly thought what would happen to them if we suddenly were sprung from the truck into their midst. Grenades thrown in all directions and then trigger happy troops running amok. It would be small consolation that any carnage inflicted would have been the direct result of the initial action by the EOKA bomber. It might well take a lot of explaining. These thoughts crowded in on me, but I had to dismiss them and concentrate on the job in hand.

Nothing happened. We drove slowly out of the village for some distance. The truck was halted, to allow enough time to pass as if we had indeed delivered rations to the radar station. We took the chance to enjoy a smoke while our Irish fellow traveller offered his opinion that there was a better chance of a bomber striking on our return journey. The time came to put out our cigarettes and climb back into the truck. We re-entered the village and this time Stan deliberately stalled the engine in the middle of the central square. He spent five minutes trying to fire the engine with no apparent success. Meanwhile, we lay in the bottom of the truck hoping that the unhealthy engine sounds would bring the bomber out to play. At one point a Cypriot woman appeared on a balcony to shake a rug. She glanced downwards as she did so at the truck below her. I had turned to cover this unexpected movement on my side. The shock was clearly registered on the woman's face as she looked down on this truck bristling with reclining soldiers and she darted back inside. Stan by this time had left his cab and was fiddling below the bonnet. After a time he got back into the cab, and this time the engine fired into life. We drove slowly out of the village without further incident, which left us somewhat deflated. As we came back into Nicosia the truck stopped and with a brisk "So Long" our Irish passenger nipped over the tailgate and disappeared quickly up the same side street that he had emerged from. We guessed that he must have been the Special Branch or some such outfit. We heard no more about any further Q-ship enterprise, but in due course Stan Wardlaw was awarded a Mention in Despatches.

In late September Gog decided that a company day out in Famagusta would be in order. We were trucked across the barren wastes of the Mesaoria, past the village where Whitton had had his chute stolen during the Company drop earlier in the summer. It still rankled with him that he had forked out financially for this theft, so he took his revenge by standing up in the truck and mooning as we roared through the village to the astonishment of the onlooking villagers.

We reached Famagusta by mid morning and looked forward to a relaxing day on Golden Sands beach. Early afternoon found a group of us diving off a raft some 100 yards or so off shore. We spotted a huge aircraft carrier anchored some distance away and it looked so near that you felt you could almost touch it. Jim Bromilow suggested that we swim out and take a closer look, so about six of us set off towards the carrier. The others were all strong swimmers and especially Bromilow who had swum at County level back in England, and soon left me behind. I ploughed on until eventually I found myself all alone in a sea with increasing size of waves. A sense of panic struck me as I realised that I was literally out of my depth. I turned for home and battled away for some considerable time. Now and again a wave would lift me up and I would get a glimpse of the beach and it seemed to get no nearer. I was aware that either I was tiring, or that currents were pulling me further out to sea, and my sense of panic increased accordingly. I gritted my teeth and put my head down and for about quarter of an hour swam as forcefully as I could towards the distant shore.

When I judged that the quarter of an hour was up, I breasted a wave to see just where I was. My worst fears were realised as I saw that the beach was as far away as ever. I trod water for a while to gather some more strength and I realised that at this rate I was most unlikely to ever make the shore. I had visions of my parents getting a War Office telegram informing them of my watery end off Golden Sands beach. Then as another wave raised me up I saw some distance away a chap in a canoe heading for the distant beach. I shouted, or rather croaked, to draw his attention but to no avail. He was bent flailing away with his paddles and heading away from me. I summoned up a last desperate roar and to my intense relief he looked back, but had some difficulty in spotting me in the now very choppy sea. I shouted again and raised my hand and this time he saw me and turned back in my direction. As he drew alongside I had recovered my composure and said to him almost conversationally "Think I've got a touch of cramp!" "O.K." he responded "Hang on to the back of the canoe–I'll get you back to shore, but it will be hard going as we are going against the currents!" "Tell me about it!" I said to myself as I clung onto the stern of the canoe, as my saviour bent to the task of getting us back to shore. When we reached the shallows I thanked my rescuer and staggered ashore to where the rest of 'C' Company were sunbathing on the sand. "Hey, where the f**k did you get to?" Bromilow enquired of me

"We had to turn back when we hit some currents out there. Don't tell me that you made it to the carrier?" "Of course I did!" I lied with a fine touch of bravado "We Scots are not frightened off by bloody currents and such like!". I made a mental note never to go swimming with Bromilow again.

In late October my mother wrote to me enclosing a cutting from our local paper "The Inverness Courier" about an Inverness man killed in Cyprus. My father on his insurance rounds in Inverness had spotted a sign outside a newsagents shop in Eastgate. It read "INVERNESS MAN KILLED IN CYPRUS". He had a dreadful premonition that something had happened to me, and could not bring himself to buy the paper. He returned home that night fully expecting to find a War Office telegram waiting for him. The cutting however was about an Inverness marine Alastair Macdougall, aged 20 years who had been killed in an EOKA ambush. His death became EOKA's 126th British victim. My parents' relief was tinged with sadness that another family had suffered such a loss.

With Famagusta and the Q-Ship operation under our belts, we felt that things were moving apace. This was underlined on 3rd November when the whole battalion was assembled to be addressed by General Ken Darling, newly appointed Director of Operations in Cyprus. We had been earmarked to take part in an active operation against EOKA and General Darling was about to explain our role in the forthcoming "Operation Filter Tip".

CHAPTER 11

CYPRUS
OPERATION 'FILTER TIP'

November 1958

"The Fox in her sleep always dreams of Chickens"

Turkish Cypriot Proverb

General Kenneth Darling who came to address the assembled ranks of 1 Para that day in early November had a considerable airborne pedigree. He transferred to the newly formed Parachute Regiment in early 1944 just in time to take part in the airborne assault on Normandy in June 1944. Although wounded early in the action, he discharged himself from a British hospital and quickly returned to his unit. In September 1944 he took command of the 12th Battalion to lead it through the Ardennes crisis in the winter of 1945 and the advance thereafter through war-torn Germany to Wismar on the Baltic Sea.

After the war there was a very real danger that the entire airborne organisation could be phased out. Darling became a leading figure in the fight to put the Regiment on a permanent footing. To this end he became the first Regimental Colonel appointed to command the Depot and regimental base at Aldershot. An important event in pursuit of recognition was the presentation of Colours by King George VI to the three regular Battalions.

General Darling's appointment as Director of Operations (Cyprus) took place significantly just one week after Mrs Cutliffe's murder.

Some 900 men of 1 Para gathered in the sunlit square to be addressed by this legendary airborne character. He stood on the back of a jeep, a stocky and pugnacious figure, and his address to us was just as uncompromising.

He stated that it gave him considerable pleasure to look out on a highly trained bunch of Paratroopers and that he wanted us to help him smash EOKA once and for all. "I'm not interested in terrorists–only in dead terrorists!" he declared.

The forthcoming operation that we would be involved in was to be called "Operation Filter Tip" and was designed in the first instance to clean out EOKA from the Kyrena range. Once that had been achieved we would push on to the Troodos Mountains to complete the task. We were left in no doubt that Darling meant business! Rumour had it that in one camp that he had addressed, young troops going out on patrol were shown the dead body of one of their comrades killed the day before.

There was very little effort made at any time to explain to us troops the real background to the Cyprus Troubles.

Long before we were called out to Cyprus I had read avidly and researched to know better the history behind the ongoing crisis. It seemed to me that the Cypriots had been, to say the least, misled by a succession of British politicians. Starting with Prime Minister Gladstone in 1897 who stated in Parliament that he hoped that Cyprus would become a Greek island in the near future. This theme was taken further by Winston Churchill some ten years later when he said: "It is right and natural for Cyprus to belong to Greece; the Cypriots' patriotic devotion to what they call their Motherland is an ideal to be cherished". This sentiment was pushed aside as the Government declared that Cyprus was not theirs to give away as it was held in trusteeship for the Turkish people. However, in 1914, after Turkey had entered World War 1 on the side of Germany the island was annexed. It was later offered to Greece if she joined the Allies– she did–but somehow Cyprus became a Crown Colony.

Matters drifted on for decades with the Greek Cypriots agitating for ENOSIS or Union with Greece. ENOSIS a dream and a political device for most of the Cypriots, but to the smaller and indigenous Turkish community an intolerable threat. With mainland Turkey only 40 miles away there was no way they wished to become a province of another, and not too affluent, a country like Greece that lay hundreds of miles away.

So in the 1950's the stage was well and truly set for matters to come to a head. It came when Britain withdrew from Suez and set up a new military HQ on Cyprus. Minister of State for Colonial Affairs, Mr. Henry Hopkinson, said that there would be no question of any change in British rule over Cyprus. In short: "Cyprus would never hope to become fully independent or to decide her own future". "I do not" added Mr. Hopkinson "see any reason to expect any difficulties in Cyprus as a result of this statement!" Greece promptly formally claimed the right of self-determination for Cypriots at a United Nations debate in December. However, in Cyprus, a hard core decided to take matters into their own hands. An organisation called EOKA (Greek for National Organisation of Cypriot Combatants) was formed. It was set up on a strictly secret basis, with cells formed in various areas and villages. Each cell was self contained with only the leader knowing the leader of the next cell so that any informer could not dismantle the entire network. Each member had to swear an oath–which went as follows:

THE OATH OF EOKA

'I swear in the name of the Holy Trinity that I . . . . shall never reveal to anyone any secrets of our Organisation, neither the name of the Leader nor that of any members, even if I am caught and tortured. If I betray–I shall deserve every punishment meted out to me and may eternal contempt cover me'.

The person chosen to lead EOKA was a retired and disgruntled former Greek Army Officer–one George Theodorou Grivas now in his late fifties. A Cypriot himself by birth, he had been born in the village of Trikomo near Famagusta. Grivas was ideally qualified for the task in hand, as during the Greek civil war he had been something of a Guerrilla warfare specialist.

It was on the deserted shores beyond Paphos that he chose to land, one dark November night in 1954, to initiate his campaign against the British. He adopted the code name Dighenis, a legendary Greek defender of the Byzantine Empire against Moslem invaders in the 12th century.

Long before his nocturnal entry, considerable supplies of arms and explosives had been secretly shipped into Cyprus and stored ready for the onset of terrorist activity. One other important figure loomed large on the Cyprus stage, that of Archbishop Makarios. Makarios, whose birth name was Mouskos, was born in the Troodos Mountains and his father was a poor shepherd. Makarios entered Kykko Monastery and brilliant scholarships took him abroad to study in Athens and America. In 1950 he became Archbishop at the early age of 37 years and tradition made him the Ethnarch, national as well as religious, spokesman for the Greek Cypriot people. It was no secret that Makarious gave tacit support to the outlawed EOKA Organisation. Rioting broke out in December 1954 when Greek youths tore down the Union Jack on the Police station at Limassol and in its place raised the Greek national flag. Two rioters were shot when British Forces were ordered to fire on the crowd. The situation gradually deteriorated until in November 1955 the then Governor Sir John Harding declared a State of Emergency throughout the island. In March 1956 Archbishop Makarios was deported to exile in the Seychelles Islands as, in the words of Sir John Harding, "He was a major obstacle to a return to peaceful conditions".

Later that month, Sir John discovered that he had spent the night sleeping on a time bomb. A Government House servant–an EOKA sympathiser–had placed it under his bed in an assassination attempt. Fortunately, the timer had proved faulty and the device was removed and exploded harmlessly in the grounds of Government House.

The crisis developed apace with repeated murders of British servicemen as the authorities struggled to bring the situation under control.

This then was the background to the Operation that we were about to embark on. We were briefed by our individual Company commanders. The Operation was designed to tackle EOKA on their own terms. Two rifle companies of 1 Para were to infiltrate the Kyrenia Range in small groups of five to six men. These groups were to lie up in different selected areas throughout the Range and monitor all movement. This information would be fed back by radio to a central command post and then relayed to an Intelligence room in Nicosia. This way a complete picture of all movement on Kyrenia Range would be obtained. It was a well established fact that villagers were giving active support to the hard core terrorists hiding in the hills.

To get that number of troops into the hills without raising undue suspicion created a problem. This was solved by using the permanent Company rest camp on the Kyrenian coast. A Company would set off ostensibly to use the camp, but at night, under the cover of darkness, the majority took off for the hills. Next day the balance of the company left in the rest camp would return to Camp Whittington and another Company would take its place.

On the night we headed for the hills we were laden with all necessary equipment and rations in bergens and set off about midnight. It was no easy task scaling the steep hillside in total darkness heading by compass for our selected area. After two hours of such climbing, we reached our area and prepared our hide. When dawn finally broke over the Kyrenian Range we saw that we were on a high point overlooking the village of Trimithi and the roads leading from it.

A routine was quickly sorted out and we took stags observing the village and roads with binoculars and logging all movement no matter how unimportant it seemed. A log was maintained and every hour this log would be relayed to our command post. Such entries as 'Man in red shirt leaves Trimithi with laden donkey at 10.15 hrs'. When the man in the red shirt passed from our sight he would be picked up by yet another observation post and his progress duly plotted.

Life became understandably a bit tedious, but we realised that it was an important part of the overall operation. We dined off Army rations, but the main problem was water, as there is no water supply in the range. Our supply was delivered by our Colour Sergeant 'Mick' Biggs who dropped off several black Jerry cans of water at designated spots along the main Kyrenia road. We had to collect these Jerry cans of water and get them back up to our Company HQ, not only for our own use, but so that other groups could be supplied as well.

On our first trip down to the coastal road I went along with Paddy. We slithered down the hillside taking as much cover as we could until we reached the roadside water drop. This was next to an olive orchard, and not far away were a Cypriot family engaged in collecting the olive harvest. The man would strike the branches with long sticks to dislodge the olives while women and children collected the fallen fruit in wicker baskets. Tethered close by were several mules saddled with two large pannier baskets to transport the collected harvest back home. We managed to avoid detection and loaded a full Jerry can into our bergen carrier and carried the other. It was hard going in the extreme, climbing back up the hill with this load and carrying a weapon into the bargain. We eventually staggered back into our hide, sweat stained and well and truly knackered.

Three days later the water run had to be done again and this time Gog selected Dave Bushell and I for the task.

We crawled down to where our Colour Sergeant had dropped off the Jerry cans of water. I was not looking forward to the return trip and a plan had hatched in my mind, and during our descent I explained it to Dave.

We collected the Jerry cans at the appointed spot, but this time I crawled forward to check on our olive pickers. They were hard at work at the far end of the orchard and well away from the spot where the donkeys were tethered under the shade of an ancient gnarled tree. I crawled across the open ground towards the mules. They were nibbling away at some wisps of hay scattered beside them, tossing their heads and occasionally stamping their hooves against the flies that bothered them. They eyed me curiously as I slithered towards them. Selecting the one that looked the most docile, I carefully unhitched its reins. Once released I led her off to where Bushell crouched with the collection of Jerry cans. The panniers on either side were ideal for housing the Jerry cans, and once loaded up we set off on the return journey. I was leading the mule holding the reins while Dave walked behind with a stick in his hand in case we had to encourage the animal. The mule proved to be an excellent choice and tackled the steep slopes with a sure footed will. As we neared the hide we unloaded the Jerry cans into our bergens and released our pack animal with a grateful slap on its rump. The mule trotted away while we headed for our hide. Gog was amazed at the good time we had made and how fresh we were. Three days later Bushell and Steel went on the water run. On the way down Bushell explained to Steel how a spot of mule rustling would make light work of the job in hand. They were to be disappointed. The Cypriot family wary of losing another mule had posted an ancient grandfather type to stand guard on their animals. So it was a long, arduous trek back up the hillside to the hide for the two frustrated would-be mule rustlers.

I did not help matters over the next few days by singing snatches from the Frankie Laine song 'Mule Train' from time to time.

By this time the intelligence gathering side of the operation had run its course. We moved in one morning just before dawn on the village of Karmi. The village was surrounded and then we moved in giving a nasty early morning call to all males over sixteen years of age. They were rounded up and taken down to an open area in the grounds of the village school. We then mounted a guard on the 200 or so males who sat on the ground in detention. In the early afternoon a police vehicle drew up close to our assembled prisoners. Inside the jeep was an EOKA informer who had been persuaded to reveal the members of the Karmi cell that he knew. The Karmi villagers were paraded one by one in front of the vehicle for the informer to identify them, although at no time was he visible to them. In the end some eight males had been identified and taken away for further questioning. The others were then released and the village put under curfew.

We carried out a similar process in various villages throughout the Kyrenian range as the EOKA cells were dismembered.

Success followed quickly. On 15th November an important EOKA member Andreas Georghiou Sofokleous was wounded and captured by a 1 Para patrol while hiding in a well in the village of Ayios Yorgios. On our side Private Johnson was caught in an ambush between Dhavlos and Kantara and had his leg blown off.

Three days later on 19th November a patrol from 'D' Company recorded the main success of the operation when the designated leader of EOKA in the Kyrenian region was killed. Kyriakos Christoforou Matsis was discovered in the cellar of a house in Drikomo along with two fellow terrorists. They surrendered, but Matsis elected to shoot it out in a brave but futile last stand and was shot and finished off with a grenade.

Mopping up continued for at least another month as the EOKA presence in the Range was effectively wiped out.

We based our Company HQ in the coffee house of Trimithi village. From this base we continued to maintain curfews on nearby villages and mount night time ambushes on the tracks leading from the villages to the high tops so as to cut off any support that the villagers might try to give to any hard core terrorists still at large.

Night ambushes could be boring in the extreme and after the warmth of the day it was surprising how cold it could become once the sun had set.

We had one luxury to help pass the long silent hours as we lay chilled to the bone in our ambush position. This took the form of a tin of self heating soup. As clearly it was impossible to cook food during an ambush, the self heating tin of soup proved a real godsend. The tin had a central core of some slow burning substance. Once two holes had been pierced in the lid, a match applied to a small wick caused the central core to smoulder slowly, heating the soup in the process. We could shelter under the cover of our ground sheet as we struck the match and then the soup tin could be put to one side to allow the heating process to take part. A further bonus was that you could warm your chilled hands on the slowly heating soup tin. In ten minutes time or so you were able to enjoy a piping hot tin of soup under the stars.

An ambush usually comprised four soldiers and, in addition to our own weapon, we carried a Greener shotgun into the bargain. In the darkness when an accurate shot might be difficult, the shot gun would hit a wider target area.

One night we had been maintaining an ambush position high on the hills above Karmi on a particularly steep part of the track. As dawn broke after another fruitless cold night and the early morning mist was lifting up the hillside as the sun rose on another Cyprus day, Paddy Tomkins, Dave Bushell and I prepared to pack up our night time vigil. We were looking forward to getting back to the coffee house HQ in the village for breakfast and a couple of hours sleep. Suddenly, out of the mist loomed Captain Grant, our Company Commander who had taken it on himself to make a snap inspection of one of his ambush positions. He was critical of where we had sited the ambush and various other aspects, and we heard him out politely, knowing full well that he was trying to impress us with empty words. We all set off down the hillside in single file with Paddy leading the way. At a certain point on the descent route we had to swing away from the direct line of the village so as to avoid a steep cliff face. Our Captain Grant was having none of it. "Cpl Tomkins" he called out "Don't go that way–this is more direct–always follow the goat tracks because they know the shortest route". "Right Sir!" said Paddy resignedly and we started to follow the narrow rutted goat track along the cliff face. At one point Captain Grant knelt down and picked up some goat droppings, crumbled them in his cupped hand and sniffed them. "What the f***k does he think he is?" hissed Bushell in my ear "Some kind of f***ing Apache scout!" Dave was clearly not too pleased at the prospect of a delayed breakfast.

The goat track wound its way round the cliff face in a very alarming fashion. At one point we were some eighty feet up on the cliff face while down below us yawned a vast scree slope where over the years erosion had dislodged large slabs of stone from the cliff face.

As we approached an outcrop in the cliff face, Paddy suddenly stopped abruptly and knelt down with raised hand. We did likewise and safety catches were released on our weapons. "What's up?" whispered Captain Grant after an interval. Paddy turned his head "Track's gone, Sir". We closed in on him, and looking over his shoulder, we could see that about twelve feet of the narrow goat track had disappeared completely leaving an unbridgeable gap. Clearly erosion had taken its toll on this part of the exposed cliff. As we were taking stock of this new situation Paddy glanced downwards. "The track's maybe gone, Sir–but I think we've caught up with them bloody goats!" he gestured, and looking down the gap we could make out away down on the scree slope the carcasses of at least three goats who had come to an untimely end. Their rib bones and skulls bleached white stood out in stark contrast to the reddish rocks of the scree. It was a much more subdued Company Commander who followed as we retraced our steps back along the cliff face with Bushell sniffing his displeasure at every opportunity. We were brewing up breakfast in Karmi coffee shop a little later when the OC's batman came in to take some tea to his lord and master.

Paddy suggested to the batman that he ask the OC if he would like some goats milk in his tea as a special treat. The batman went off in all innocence to offer this special treat to the OC and returned pretty sharpish with a sizeable flea in his ear! It did not make him feel any better when the coffee shop rocked with coarse laughter.

Regular patrolling in the area turned up two hides in the Karmi area with ammunition and explosives stored ready for use. In Trimithi another hide was located that yielded a shotgun with 150 rounds and a supply or cordite.

A week or so after the death of Matsis our earlier intelligence gathering paid dividends. A more modern style bungalow outside Ayios Georgios was found to have a secret cellar. Entry was gained by raising a disguised flagstone in the kitchen which led to the underground cellar that held a large bomb ready for use. We were called out to guard the premises while bomb disposal experts from Nicosia were summoned to look into the matter. The bomb expert had a good long look at it before emerging with his findings. The bomb had indeed been completed, but was too big to be removed from the cellar. "Bloody EOKA must be employing an Irish bomb-maker now!" was his comment. An observation that Paddy Tomkins took strong exception to!

As the house owner had been taken away for questioning, and his family dispersed, the decision was taken to blow the bomb up in situ–and the bungalow along with it! We withdrew to a safe distance and the bomb detonated. It was quite a spectacle as the bungalow flew skywards under the force of the explosion. The blackened and ruined site would serve as a deterrent to any other bomb making specialist.

"Better here than in some street in Nicosia!" was the final comment passed by the mild looking bespectacled bomb disposal expert. People generally think that Paras are endowed with their fair share of courage, but for my money, the bomb disposal boys are in a league of their own.

Two days later we were maintaining a curfew on the village of Lapithos to the west of Kyrenia town. This involved us in 'soft shoe' patrolling of the village and again in laying up overnight ambushes on roads leading from the village. We had been doing this for a couple of nights and returning to our coffee house base at breakfast time. There, after a quick meal we would clean our weapons and try to grab a couple of hours sleep in a sleeping bag on the hard stone paved flooring of the coffee shop. The weapons, after cleaning, were stored in a far corner of the coffee shop well away from the open door. The magazines would be removed and placed beside them.

That night we were preparing to set off for a new ambush position. With blackened faces we collected our weapons and were poring over a map to determine our proposed new ambush position. I had collected my rifle from the Arms store in the corner and was about to slip the magazine into position when I noticed that the bolt of my rifle was not fully home, or as we called it, at 'half cock'. This could sometimes happen during the cleaning process and, simply by pressing the trigger, the bolt would click fully home. So with the full magazine in my left hand, and cradling my rifle in my right hand, I proceeded to do just that. With some difficulty, as others crowded round the map on the table, I raised the rifle and pointed it towards the roof before pulling the trigger.

What I was not to know was that a live round nestled in the chamber of my rifle! During the day it was standard practice for any of us to be called on armed escort duty on any military vehicle heading for Kyrenia or Nicosia. This duty was called 'riding shotgun'. Most military vehicles on duty in Cyprus had been adapted for this with a large roundel cut in the roof. The armed escort stood up in the vehicle with the upper part of his body sticking out of the roof holding his weapon at the ready.

Earlier that day Steel had been called upon to ride shotgun on the OC champ en route to a briefing in Nicosia. Somewhere along the road he had occasion to put a round into the barrel in case of an emergency. On his return he replaced my rifle where he had found it and laid the magazine beside it, quite forgetting that he had a deadly round up the spout!

I pressed the trigger confidently expecting a satisfying click as the bolt went home. The rifle explosion, as the round tore into the ceiling of the coffee shop, was ear splitting in the confined and crowded room! I stood in dumb amazement looking in total disbelief from my smoking weapon in one hand, to my magazine clutched in the other. The others in the room were shocked into a strange silence.

This was broken abruptly when the coffee house door crashed open and Paddy Tomkins shot into the room at top speed. He was heading for the weapon store in the corner when he came to an abrupt halt at the sight of the silenced room, and me standing there with literally a smoking rifle in my hands.

Paddy had been sitting outside up on the flat roof of the coffee shop. His job was to maintain radio communication with all the various patrol units out in the field by means of an 88 set radio. He had been leaning forward fiddling with the controls when suddenly a large piece of roofing between his legs was blown up to the accompaniment of a rifle shot. Naturally, Paddy assumed that an EOKA sniper had opened up on him and, with no personal weapon to hand, he was off the roof faster than a tom cat on heat!

As it dawned on Paddy that far from being target practise for EOKA he had come under friendly fire–he was not amused! There followed some heated observations on my abilities as a soldier along with the legitimacy of my ancestors.

The Army teaches one to respect weapons at all times and never to assume anything without checking, and I had been taught a sharp reminder. To his credit, Steel apologised later, but the damage was done– but it could have been much worse!

As the Operation was dragging to a close we were allowed to go back in batches of four in a jeep back to Camp Whittington for the sheer luxury of a shower and a cooked meal. One Sunday as some of us were preparing to head off on a 24 hour break, Paddy decided that it would be a good idea en route to stop for Mass at the Catholic church in Nicosia. So four of us of that persuasion broke the journey to join the congregation. A congregation that was mainly composed of Service people, so that we would not feel out of place in our uniforms. It turned out to be not such a bright idea from our section commander. The church was crowded with little or no ventilation and after our days in the hills, unwashed and without a change of clothing, our personal freshness was somewhat in question. To be brutally frank–we stank!–and some people around us seemed to have bad colds as they made much use of the handkerchiefs.

The cold primitive showers back in Camp Whittington did wonders for our morale. It was also a time for catching up with the news. A new Pope– Pope John XXII had been crowned early in the month which came as a surprise to us. In Paris de Gaulle had invested Winston Churchill with the

Cross of Lorraine and the Order of Liberation–a bit late in the day we thought–but then better late than never.

Paddy Tomkins had a veritable cascade of letters from his Maree which kept him quiet for some time. The Inverness Courier informed me that there had been a sighting of the Loch Ness Monster towards the end of the tourist season and that Hugh Fraser the brother of Lord Lovat had been given a junior government post in a reshuffle. Appointed along with him were two politicians unknown to me John Profumo and Julian Amery.

A relaxing night at the open air cinema and a good sleep in our tent bed and next morning we were ready to head back to the hills.

Shortly after we came back one night, we were approached on a soft shoe patrol by a distressed Cypriot who claimed his child was very ill. He begged us to see our officer to get permission to take the sick child to the local church for a blessing. Gog agreed to this and Paddy and I were detailed to escort the couple to the church. There the bearded priest met with them, and in the dim candlelight church, prayers were intoned over the sick child wrapped in a blanket in his mother's arms. We sat in the back of the church with our weapons well out of sight. When the short service was concluded we escorted the two parents back to their home. The baby did not survive the night and next day four of us were detailed to provide the funeral escort to the local graveyard. We met up at the house. The father emerged carrying the small corpse wrapped and tied in a sort of white winding sheet. The mother was one of a group of some thirty women who made up the openly grieving cortege. We had to walk about half a mile to the graveyard which was situated high above the village. Once there the father and two elderly men set about digging a grave, while the women sat some distance away weeping and wailing. The parched earth was hard and stony and the diggers were making heavy weather of creating the grave. We took over to speed things up and soon one of the old men decided that the grave was sufficiently deep for the interment.

The wrapped body of the dead infant was placed in the grave and the earth quickly filled in without much ceremony. The women performed the final act by placing large stones over the stony raised mound We felt that we should do something to show our respect as well, and it was Griffin who suggested that we observe a minute's silence. We removed our berets and stood in silence round the fresh grave–a somewhat strange collection of mourners–a South African, and Englishman, an Irishman and a Scotsman acknowledging the brief life that had just been ended. This done we escorted the funeral party back down the road to their homes in the village. The father insisted we share a glass of Commanderia wine with him before we took our leave.

Next day it was back to business as normal. Trimithi was the setting for a mock funeral in honour of the late Matsis. We were called in to disperse the congregation after the service and came in for a fierce bout of stoning from the womenfolk. One of our lot Private 'Gungy' Gordon got detached from us during the melee. Gungy got his name due to the fact that although he came from Glasgow, he was not of pure Scottish stock. At a rough guess he was possibly three quarter Scot and one quarter African, and this cultural confusion had left him with a swarthy complexion. A splinter group of the roused congregation closed in on him intent on wrecking severe bodily harm. However Gungy was a battle scarred veteran of many an Aldershot pub brawl and was equal to the occasion. He simply fixed his bayonet and cut and slashed his way back to the relative safety of our main body. The men folk sheltered behind the stone throwing harridans so we had to perform one or two snatch assaults to remove the ring leaders before peace and quiet was restored.

It was later revealed that one of the reasons that the congregation got so inflamed was due to the fact that the collection plate of money had disappeared. It was clear that certain members of 'C' Company could never change their spots.

Later patrols were still meeting with success in detecting hidden EOKA hides–one south of Karmi yielded a rifle and an amount of ammunition.

In early December we were told that Operation Filter Tip had run its course and we were all returning to civilisation in the shape of Camp Whittington.

General Darling expressed his thanks to all ranks of 1 Para for the resounding success of the past couple of months.

As battalion life in Camp Whittington returned to normality, it was time for all those who had fallen foul of military discipline to account for their sins. This took the shape of appearing before the Commanding Officer. About sixty of us stood to attention on this parade of miscreants while RSM Bromley prowled among us looking for minor defects in our uniforms and general appearance. A fine mist was rolling in heralding the start of the rainy season and this had the effect of having an itching effect as it settled on your face. Standing to attention it was a difficult decision to resist wiping it away, as the fine moisture ran down your face. Well not too difficult a decision as it would have brought down the wrath of RSM Bromley which was to be avoided at all costs.

Eventually it was my time to be marched in to face Lt Col Reinhold our Commanding Officer.

Standing before him, stiffly to attention, while the RSM shouted out the details of my crime. When he had finished the CO said quietly "How do you answer the charge?" "Guilty as charged Sir!" I fired back. "Have you nothing to say in mitigation of this serious charge?" probed the CO. "It would take too long to relate–and would not alter the fact, Sir". The CO slowly stood up and crossed to the window of the office and looked out. He slowly turned his head and said to me "Come over here, Grant". I joined him at the window. Looking across the neat rows of tents you could make out the military cemetery through the green trees that lined the plot. The rich brown earth of a freshly dug grave was only too clearly evident. The Co gestured in that direction. "Do you realise that your action could have resulted in one of your comrades being buried in that very grave?". I had visions of Gog ordering me to write to Paddy's Maree to try and explain to her how I had blasted her fiancé into eternity from the roof of a coffee house. "Yes, Sir" I said contritely with enough gravity in my voice to impress him. "Very well. One week's stoppage of pay Sergeant Major" was the verdict of the CO as he returned to his desk seat.

"DISMISS–ABOUT TURN ...." Hollered the RSM as he marched me out of the office and back into the criminal ranks.

The punishment was light as we had not been paid during our stint on Operation Filter Tip and several weeks pay had accrued.

There was to be no rest for us as word came that we were pulling out of Camp Whittington for a new base in the Troodos Mountains in the south. We were to be deployed on a similar type of role against EOKA to see if we could repeat the success that we had achieved on the Kyrenian Range.

CHAPTER 12

CYPRUS
OPERATION MARE'S NEST

December 1958–March 1959

"So long as he has a tooth left in his head a Fox won't be pious!"
Greek Cypriot Proverb

As we prepared to take our leave of Camp Whittington a debriefing took place on the recently concluded "Operation Filter Tip" to see what lessons could be learned that might assist us in the Troodos. I am not sure how much good it did in that respect, but it certainly turned up one or two classic yarns. The best in my opinion was turned in by 3 Platoon of 'A' Company. On 22nd November a patrol was investigating a movement of wooden crates from a green van to a house. An old Cypriot man came forward to volunteer the information that the house was full of EOKA. The patrol went into action convinced that they were about to take out the HQ of the EOKA Kyrenian organisation. They stormed the house only to find no incriminating evidence of any kind. The elderly informer was then taken to Tactical HQ for further questioning by an interpreter. Once there the old man made a clean breast of things. He admitted that he had sent the patrol to the house on the off chance that they might shoot his seventy one year old uncle who was supposed to be carrying on an affair with his wife!

Once back in Camp after the weeks of non stop action in the hills a certain soldier, again in 'A' Company, wrote to the Daily Sketch in an idle moment. "Two lonely Paratroopers fighting in Cyprus would like girl pen friends". The result was that the Company postal office was bombarded with hundreds of replies of which only three had photos and about a hundred had either insufficient or no postage!

On the 14th December 1 Para bade fond farewell to Camp Whittington which had been our base ever since arriving in July. We travelled south in a fleet of three tonners towards the distant mass of the Troodos Mountains to relieve 45 Marine Commando.

101

Winter was late in coming in 1958 and for the first couple of weeks we were blessed with summer like weather. This was just as well as our MT drivers were initiated into the art of driving on the steep tortuous mountain roads without the additional hazards of snow and ice. That being said, one or two wandered off the road but fortunately there were no fatalities.

The winding roads with pine tree forests made me think that I was back in the Cairngorms. The various rifle companies of 1 Para were scattered throughout the Troodos area. 'A' Company were allotted the Mount Olympus-Agros-Alona District: Support Company took up residence in the Pinewood Camp area while 'C' Company took over the dilapidated Hotel Neptune in the village of Platres. It was an hotel in name only as it was just a bare uncarpeted shell of a building and most certainly no 5 Star hospitality on offer. A small rear party of Marines were still in Platres sorting out things as the main body had left for Malta. As it was late at night when we arrived we settled down for the night in the room recently vacated by the Marines.

Some hours later I was awakened from a deep sleep to find myself being beaten up in my bed! I had no sensation of pain as I awoke to see a dark burly figure standing by my bed raining down blows on me. I came to life in an instant and lashed out with my feet sending my assailant crashing to the floor. Leaping out of my bed I pinned him to the floor wondering how many other EOKA members were close by. The noise roused the rest of the sleeping billet and when the lights were switched on we were more than surprised to find that my captor was one very drunk Marine. It turned out that my bed had been his original bed space and in his drunken condition he had wandered back to his old billet, only to find his bed occupied. It was a welcome to Platres that I could have well done without! Next day one of our three tonners driven by Van Wyk with Paddy Kelly as escort was blown up by an electronically detonated mine. Severely wounded they were both shipped off to hospital in Akrotiri to recover before being flown home.

We quickly settled into life in Troodos and a pattern of manning observation hides and our favourite pastime of ambushing was established, supported by foot patrols and road checks. Christmas was celebrated as best we could and one of the few highlights was a very successful record programme staged by 'C' Company and HQ Company on the Cyprus Broadcasting Network. The programme was introduced by Ptes Kelly and Van Dyk recovering from their wounds in hospital and compered by L/Cpl Paddy Tomkins and my old Orderly Room friend Pte Goldsack.

Apart from a festive type meal Christmas for most of us was just another working day but we looked forward to a two day rest period to celebrate the New Year.

It turned out to be a big mistake because there was little to do in Platres village except to drink. A couple of hundred troops cooped up in a barbed wire compound and fuelled by drink was just asking for trouble. The hit tune of 1958 was Perry Como singing 'Magic Moments' and for us there had been precious few magic moments over the past year and New Year's Eve was to prove no exception.

After a day of heavy imbibing, a group of us were singing our way back to our billet in Hotel Neptune very much the worse for wear. At that time I shared a room with three others namely Surtees, Steel and Bushell. As we entered the hallway of the hotel, Surtees emerged from our room to inform us that he had just had a fight with Steel. Surtees was a bully by nature and always seemed to be picking on the younger Steel. Surtees stood with his back to the bedroom door giving us details of what he had done, when just behind him appeared a bloody hand on the door jamb. Then Steel lurched into view, his face a mask of blood, with a knife in his hand. He lunged at Surtees' back with the weapon. Paddy shouted a warning and Surtees half turned so that the knife thrust missed its broad target and caught him a glancing blow on his forearm. At this all hell broke loose as various people piled in and the weapon was secured. In the melee, for no good reason, I punched in the glass of the notice board that contained Company orders badly gashing my fist in the process. Gradually order was restored and Steel was taken off to the Medical Officer's Quarters and Surtees into overnight detention. Our Platoon Sergeant 'Middie' Campbell appeared on the scene and ordered me to the MO's quarters to have my fist stitched and stem the bleeding. When law and order was restored, the billet finally settled down to sleep as the New Year of 1959 broke over the Troodos Mountains.

When I returned duly stitched up and with my hand bandaged I too settled down to sleep the sole occupant in our room as Bushell was clearly on an all night drinking session elsewhere.

There is a ritual in the Army that on New Year's morning the Company Sergeant Major dishes out morning tea to his charges just to show that he is human. Ably assisted by the Colour Sergeant, they haul round an urn of lukewarm, stewed tea and dish it out.

When Gog and Mick Biggs came into the room in the morning they nearly dropped the urn. I was lying in bed with a bandaged hand, the other beds were empty and overturned and the walls were daubed with Steel's life blood.

"Christ Almighty!" said Gog "How come you're the only f****ing survivor?" "And a Happy New Year to you, Sir!" was all I had to say as I gratefully clutched my mug of tea.

It was something of a relief to get back to normal soldiering activities. There was a trickle of men due for demob leaving our ranks and at this time we said goodbye to Ptes Denis Purton and Connolly as they headed for civvy street. Denis in particular had, like most national servicemen nearing demob, a huge calendar above his bed on which he marked off the days one by one. In the final month he had a big sign over it that read "DAYS TO DO–VERY FEW!" On the other hand Turner in the next bed to Purton had clearly got depressed at the constant reference to demob with his own release date quite some time away. The notice above his bed read "ROLL ON DEATH!–DEMOB'S TOO FAR WAY."

January saw winter break over the Troodos with a vengeance and it was reckoned to be one of the coldest on record with heavy snow falls. As Operation Mares Nest got under way we were to provide a Tactical Headquarters for an Infantry Brigade in the Kambos area of Troodos. The weather worsened with really cold and windy conditions and, as we shivered in our tent hides high on the Troodos, we thought longingly of the extremely hot conditions we had endured in the Dustbowl and Goshi just months earlier.

During this spell of bad weather, we constantly patrolled and manned observation hides and once again gave due thanks for tins of self heating soup.

One slight diversion was ski patrol training carried out on the heights of Mount Olympus. 'D' Company based in the valleys of Agros and Alona were having a rather interesting time. Their area had a reputation for being openly hostile and giving on-going support to the hard bitten and active 'andarti' or mountain terrorist groups. 1 Platoon survived an all out attack on the Police station at Agros with commendable coolness. Some weeks later 3 Platoon seized a quantity of explosives in Agros and a full scale riot developed as they closed in on the terrorist hide. A large and angry stone throwing crowd assembled and tried to pin down fourteen members of the Platoon. The tense situation developed further until 3 Platoon fixed bayonets and finally convinced them that it would be in their best interests to disperse.

Word from the outside world continued to filter our way and among the items of interest was that one Fidel Castro had seized power in Cuba, and that Mike Hawthorn the 29 year old British racing driver had been killed in a car crash on the Guildford bypass. Also on the sporting front, a 24 year old boxer from South London had won the British and Empire Heavyweight Boxing championship. His name was Henry Cooper.

The real hammer blow, news wise, came early in when we learned that Buddy Holly the highly talented American rock singer had been killed in an air crash on 3rd February. He had been on an internal flight to perform in a show in North Dakota along with Richie Valens and the 'Big Bopper' when the aircraft went down with no survivors. Buddy Holly with his band the Crickets were unique members of the early rock movement in music. He was the first pop star to compose and arrange his own hits. His backing of guitars and drums–with no brass–pioneered a new and exciting sound.

Word of this came through to us on Friday 6th February when we had it sent to us through the company 88 set radio as we sheltered in our hide, high on the Troodos, from a wintry squall. It was exactly a year to the day that the Manchester United plane had crashed in Munich.

In early February we were aware that events in Cyprus were coming to a head with the likely transformation of Cyprus into an independent state.

Patrols were run down, and more and more troops were sent on skiing trips to help fill in their days.

In London Prime Minister Harold MacMillan was entertaining Archbishop Makarios for talks on the island's future.

At this time we were told that a limited number of trips were available for those who wished to visit Jerusalem and the Holy Land. This was too good an opportunity to miss, so I quickly filed my application. Paddy Tomkins did likewise and went with three other members of 'C' Company, Cpls Jim Hunt, David 'Mitch' Mitchell and Pte Griffin. I missed out on this party and after they returned I went as part of another quartet with three members from 'A' Company.

We made the hair raising trip down the twisting Troodos roads to Nicosia airport and our trip away from the island. The aircraft, complete with charming air hostesses, was sheer luxury to us more used to the spartan conditions aboard the Hastings and Beverleys. The two hour flight took us to Jerusalem airport and we were put up at a very comfortable Church of England hostel in the heart of the old city. Just outside the hostel was the 'souk' or local market place a fascinating place to wander about in. The crowded stalls were full of gold and silver ware, rugs, fruit, meat and various other trades and overall a wonderful smell of strange spices.

The ten days spent in Jerusalem and its surrounds was an unforgettable experience. We visited all the places of tourist interest–The Dome of the Rock, The Holy Sepulchure, Mount Calvary, The Garden of Gethsemane with its ancient olive trees. Further afield we went to Bethlehem, the Shepherds Field and, of course, bathed in the Dead Sea. It was a superb change from life in Cyprus, and all too soon it came to an end. The return flight touched down at Nicosia airport and we were soon heading back up into the hills to rejoin our units.

Our Commanding Officer, Captain Grant, had left us and in his place was Major P. de M. Baynham. In addition, Lt Col Gordon Reinhold had also departed on completion of his tour of command. It was definite now in early March that 1 Para were heading home and everybody became very focused on this forthcoming event.

Fifteen worthy souls from the battalion had elected to travel home as part of an initiative exercise. Travelling in civilian clothing they intended to hitch hike home to Blighty! Their Army luggage would be taken home along with the rest of the Battalion goods and chattels. Included in this intrepid bunch were two worthies from 'C' Company–Cpl Bob Ash and Pte Phil Purkiss. Bob came into our tent one night shortly before they were about to leave to show us an exquisite and ornate silver flask of Chanel No 5 perfume that he was taking home to his wife. Naturally we got him to uncork the flask so that we could sniff its exotic contents. Bushell wound him up by saying that, passing through various customs, that each one would clobber him for excise duties that would result in costing him a fortune. This worried Bob for a while. He returned to our tent a couple of days later to say that he had solved his problem. He had a friend in the Medical Officer's staff who could get him a supply of flesh coloured elastoplast. Using this he would strap the flask to the calf of his leg and it would remain there intact until he unwrapped it once he got safely home. This he did, making a very neat and unobtrusive job of it, and we wished him God speed and all the best on his safari.

They hitched a lift to Malta in an empty Transport Command plane, crossed from there to Italy, and foot slogged it with various lifts across Europe to England and home. The story did not end happily for Bob as he was welcomed back into the bosom of his family. He unwrapped his wife's present before an admiring audience, only to find that the flask was bone dry! It appeared that the stopper had not been firmly replaced and the warmth of his leg, not to say the warm climates that they passed through, had all helped to evaporate the precious Chanel No 5. Bob took a long time to live this one down.

The battalion set off for home in the latter part of February leaving a small rear party to tidy up Camp Whittington after their phased departure. I was again on this rear party due to the fact that we had arrived in Cyprus after the main body of the battalion. I grabbed the chance to ride shotgun on a trip to Kykko Monastery. I had always wanted to see the island's most famous monastery that held a revered icon called the Elousa. I stood in the cab of the three tonner with the top half of my body exposed to the elements. The truck wound its way up from the foothills and along the twisting mountain roads with the pine forests far below us. The snow lay heavy on the hillsides and the truck had to proceed carefully on the untended roads. The cold biting wind made my eyes stream and even holding the rifle became difficult as my hands chilled. It was just as well that EOKA were lying low because of the peace process. Reduced to cradling the rifle in my arms, I would not have been in much shape to react if we had run into trouble.

Rear party became a bit of a drag as we had little to do but sit round the Waynes Keep NAAFI drinking endless cups of tea and listening to Shirley Bassey belting out her latest hit 'Kiss me, Honey, Honey, Kiss me'!

One morning as the day yawned ahead of us, I asked if anybody wanted to go with me for a last jaunt over Kyrenia to visit Bellapais village for the last time. I had only one taker–John 'Jenny' Wren a fellow 'C' Company member. Jenny was a Brummy from Birmingham. Like me, taller than the average Para, he had a heavily pock marked face and naturally husky voice which gave him an unprepossessing appearance and, in short, not somebody you would like to bump into on a dark night. Ironically he was very good natured and I always found him a reliable and interesting companion. We secured permission from the Sergeant in charge of the rear party, on the condition that we remained armed during our walk.

Jenny and I set off just after breakfast and crossed the Mesaoria, passing one or two herds of tinkling sheep, watched over by their patient shepherds. They looked at us without any show of emotion as we passed and did not return our greeting. Jenny remarked to me that he wondered if they even knew that a possible peace settlement for their island was on the way, or if they did, what they thought about it.

We walked on and once more scaled the crest of the Range with the azure sea in the distance. Down the steep slopes avoiding any village until at last we dropped into Bellapais. The village still slumbered in the sunshine and we picked our way down the street to a table under the Tree of Idleness where we ordered a welcome couple of Keo beers. The villagers who occupied the other tables studiously ignored us, even when we acknowledged them. After a while, to our surprise, one of the men rose from a table and sat down beside us with his coffee. He turned out to be the local school teacher with an excellent command of English. Why were we here he asked, as he had understood that the Paratroopers had all gone back to Britain. We explained about our presence on rear party and our wish to have a last look at Bellapais. Talk soon got on to the forthcoming peace settlement and what it would mean for the island. It will be a compromise, said the teacher. Cypriots want independence and Britain wants a Middle East military base and both will get what they want. In his opinion this could have been thrashed out a decade before and avoided all the bloodshed and bitterness on both sides. Jenny and I had to admit that we could find no fault in his argument.

I asked him if he had any fears for the future and had the Turkish minority anything to fear with independence? He said that Turkish interests would be protected in any agreement but his personal worry was that Makarios would reward some hard core terrorists with high position in the new administration, who might not share the same agenda as the wily Archbishop.

We talked and sipped coffee long into the afternoon before the time came to head back for the last time over the range and back to camp.

On 1st March we were informed that we were to depart. We were ordered to drive in civilian clothes with all Army gear packed and were driven to Nicosia airport at the unearthly hour of 5 a.m.! Even then crowds of people were out and about as Archbishop Makarios was about to make a triumphant return that very day to Nicosia. We were driven quickly to a small hut at the rear of the airport and instructed not to move from it until we were ready to board our aircraft. It was felt that, with feelings running high with the return of Makarios, that certain elements in the crowd might take strong exception to our presence.

We sat cooped up for hours in a badly ventilated hut until in early afternoon we boarded our plane for home. We were all delighted to be heading home, but I could not resist a last long look from the aircraft window as we left the sunlit island in our wake.

CHAPTER 13

RETURN TO THE U.K.

April 1959 August 1959

"In England's Green and Pleasant Land"
Blake's 'Jerusalem'

As we returned to England full details of the agreement that had ended the fighting in Cyprus were revealed. The agreement provided for a Republic to be established within a year. There would be a Greek-Cypriot President and a Turkish-Cypriot Vice-President. It ended effectively eighty years of British rule and the violence that had caused over five hundred deaths in the past four years. Just as the Bellapais school master had predicted Britain was allowed to retain her two military bases on the island and, just as ominously, some hard core members of EOKA still expressed their dissatisfaction that full ENOSIS with Greece had not been achieved.

Still that was all behind us now as we prepared to go home on a month's well earned block leave. Nothing much seemed to have changed in Aldershot, and on my way to the railway station I observed that 'The Mousetrap' was still running in the same theatre in London. My return to the UK went like a bomb–almost literally!

I caught the overnight Euston-Inverness express that was due to leave at 7 p.m. The train was crowded, but I managed to secure a window seat and settled down for the long trip north. About 9 p.m. with the journey well under way most people in the carriage started to unpack their sandwiches and thermos flasks. When we were sorting out the stores prior to leaving Wayne's Keep I had liberated two tins of self heating soup. The very same soup that had cheered and warmed us up on many a long and cold night on ambush duty in Kyrenia and elsewhere.

I was very aware as I took the tin out of my suitcase that all eyes of my fellow travellers were on me. I placed the tin on a small window ledge, prised off the cap and lit the wick. Then I settled back with a magazine giving the soup time to warm up. After a few minutes I tested the tin and found it was quite warm. Then it struck me that I had forgotten to pierce two holes in the lid before heating the soup. This was very essential as the tin was liable to explode when it got too hot! What to do? I was well aware that I had nothing in my possession capable of quickly piercing the two holes in the lid. I had to get the tin out of the compartment–and fast! I went to pick up the tin, but by now it was too hot to hold. Gripping it with my handkerchief I got out of the compartment with as much dignity as I could summon. Once in the train corridor, my first thought was to heave it out of the nearest window. But we were running slowly through a station and I could not bring myself to lob it into the midst of the waiting travellers standing there. Next best thing was a toilet–fortunately the one closest to me was free. I dived inside and placed the tin on the cistern lid, as it was now becoming too hot to hold. I then withdrew at top speed. Now the problem was that I dare not leave the toilet unattended in case some unsuspecting person strolled in and got more than they bargained for. I stood outside smoking calmly. Only one person approached to use the toilet, and I explained that my mate was inside feeling unwell and it was advisable to use another toilet.

Standing outside the toilet, with the noisy rattle of the train I was not able to hear any sound. I had visions of my parents getting a War Office telegram along the lines "The War Office regrets to inform you of the loss of your son whilst on service. It is ironic that having survived a spell of active service in Cyprus with his battalion, that he should have met his end as a result of an exploding tin of cream of mushroom soup on the overnight express to Inverness . . . ".

When I judged that it was safe to open the toilet door to investigate, I very cautiously put my head round the door. I gazed on a pretty horrendous scene. The tin had indeed exploded and the heating core had scored the ceiling, while cream of mushroom soup dripped down the four walls. Gingerly picking up the split tin, I lobbed it out of the window into the darkness and returned to my seat.

The rest of the journey was uneventful although one member who had left the carriage later to presumably go to the toilet kept giving me rather strange looks for the rest of the journey.

The four weeks leave passed only too quickly. Cyprus still featured in the news with EOKA accepting the London peace agreement and the elusive Colonel George Grivas making a triumphant return to Athens on the 17th March.

During this leave period Paddy Tomkins married his Maree with the newly demobbed Denis Purton as his best man. Dave Bushell too had been due to tie the knot about the same time.

All members of 1 Para reported back to Albuhera Barracks on 1st April to find that we had a new Commanding Officer Lt Col Awdry. Our charismatic chaplain Rev Horace McClelland had left us after five years to take up a new appointment as a chaplain to a Boys Training Battalion in Wales.

Our Company members, a bit depleted after Cyprus, were swollen by a new intake of recruits fresh from Depot. Most of them were signed for a six year term as the Paras phased out troops even on a three year engagement. This only served to remind us National Service mercenaries that we were a dying breed.

We welcomed Ptes Boswarva, Dobie, Leaver, Wilkie, Brady, Doak, Davidson and Crabbe to our ranks. They had to listen quietly while we old sweats exchanged Cyprus war stories! Anyone who imagined that returning to the UK would be more relaxing after Cyprus was wrong. Classification on the newly issued NATO weapon–the Belgian SLR rifle–proceeded apace until all ranks were happy with its use. Parachuting continuation training was very much the order of the day now. We did a company drop at Frensham during which Surtees and Carty got spectacularly tangled up in mid air and descended like a pair of Siamese twins.

On the debriefing Gog remarked sourly that although he expected his Bren gun pair to stay close together, this was carrying things a bit too far!

Paddy and his brand new wife had acquired a flat in St Michaels road so he now lived out of barracks. With less than two months to go to his demob in May he was under considerable pressure from Gog to sign on and make the Army his career. Any thought that Paddy might have entertained on this score were to be well and truly crushed in a most tragic way. It was not unknown for a soldier to leave the Regiment and then return if they found it difficult to settle in civvy street, or failed to find suitable employment. Indeed 'C' Company had just welcomed back Cpl Tom Godwin along with Ptes Rivers and Lawes. On the week of his demob Paddy had handed all his Army gear back to the Quartermaster's stores and was knocking about the billet in his civilian clothing. The morning of Wednesday 13th May found us parading outside 'C' Company block prior to heading off for a day on the shooting range. Down the lines marched the Anti Tank Platoon, weapon containers hoisted on their shoulders heading for their transport on the square taking them off to do a jump. There was as usual a bit of good natured banter as they passed us by. They were in fact taking part in a parachuting display at the Imperial Defence College at Netheravon.

In late afternoon as we returned from the ranges our Company Commander Major P. de M. Baynham was waiting for us with tragic news. A member of the Anti Tank Platoon Wille Wilson–a former member of 'C' Company–had been killed on the drop due to a parachute failure. The OC went on to tell us that next day the entire battalion would take part in what was termed as a 'confidence' jump in case anybody dwelled on the accident. Gog grabbed me to rustle up the appropriate Flight Manifest lists for the next day. To my surprise Gog had included Paddy's name on the list jumping No 5 on the port side. "Aren't you forgetting, Sir" I said drawing his attention to this error "that Cpl Tomkins has handed in all his gear to the Stores and is effectively demobbed?". "Like bloody hell he is!" retorted Gog "he is still technically in the Army so he can just bloody well draw his gear out again!"

So down on the flight manifest list went his name and I thought to myself that will be a nice little surprise for the demob happy boy come the morning.

After supper about six of us headed downtown to slake our thirsts at the Rat Pit pub. En route who should we espy across the street but Paddy and Maree heading arm in arm for a quiet night at the Regal cinema. Before I could stop him 'Wiggy' Wigham gave them a shout and crossed the street to accost him with the news. At first Paddy was convinced that we were winding him up, but when I related what Gog had said he realised it was true. Maree was meantime hanging on white faced to his arm. I knew then that any lingering idea that Paddy might have had of a return to the Paras had been well and truly knocked. Next morning Paddy had to draw out fresh gear and join our ranks once more, and we did our level best to wind him up in the back of the truck taking us to Blackbushe airport. The battalion drop onto Frensham Common went without a hitch and it was a highly relieved Paddy who handed his gear back for a second and final time.

For some of our newest recruits it was their first battalion jump and some way to launch their real jumping career. It was the normal thing for older hands to take the rise out of the new arrivals. None was more adept at this than Bob Ash if he found himself behind a slightly apprehensive new jumper. He carried a length of parachute strop with a frayed end inside his denison jacket for this purpose. When 'Action Stations' came and everybody hooked up and stood in line facing the door with the red light on, Bob would tap the new jumper on the shoulder to get his attention above the roar of the engines. The newcomer would turn his head to see what Bob wanted and this was the cue for Bob to show him the frayed strop length as if it came from the newcomer's chute and shout "Think you've got a bit of a problem here, mate!"

The newcomer naturally would get more than a bit agitated knowing that the green light was due to go at any moment until at the last moment Bob would stick the strop length back inside his smock and the floor show would be over–until next time.

As Paddy marched off into civvy street, life in the Battalion went on. The Battalion had a notable success when our Adjutant Captain Orphen-Smellie distinguished himself as a marksman at Bisley. Field training took up much of our time at this period and an inter company fire and movement competition was won by 'C' Company's Cpl George Brown. It was clear that George was on a fairly fast track through the ranks. Apart from being a first class soldier George proved to be an equally good off duty companion. We shared a mutual love of football and as Scots we took a lot of stick in April when England defeated Scotland 1–0 at Hampden Park in the annual match. The winning goal was scored by none other than Bobby Charlton.

When finances were tight George and I would make do on a Saturday with supporting lowly Aldershot F.C. from the terraces. After the match we would head as often as not to the main NAAFI Club down town for a supper before heading back to the billet. The centre piece of the Club was a huge juke box that belted out the latest popular hits. A play cost sixpence and it would accept ten selections in advance. The juke box catered for all musical tastes and at that time Jimmy Shand the revered Scottish dance band leader had a catchy number called 'Whistling Rufus' in the lower reaches of the Hit Parade. George would carefully select "Whistling Rufus" for the maximum ten consecutive turns. This done we ordered our supper and sat back to enjoy the fun. 'Whistling Rufus' would come on play–go off–come back on again–play–go off and so on. About half way through our programme the large restaurant would be in some kind of an uproar as Jimmy Shand tied up the juke box and many diners reacted noisily at this overdose of Scottish musical culture.

Late May saw parachute training continue with an accident free night drop at Everleigh. This was followed by Exercise 'Full House' on Salisbury Plain. This took the shape of a drop followed by an Inter Platoon competition among the three rifle companies involving a 56 mile 'tab' or route march back to Aldershot with two overnight halts in bivouac areas. Early June in glorious weather saw 'C' Company down at the School of Infantry in Warminster for our role in their annual demonstration. 7 Platoon did the static demonstration on the square whilst the remainder of the company did the parachute descent. For this we had to travel to RAF Lyneham to board our Beverleys. As a special treat because 'C' Company had just won the Battalion Champion Company competition Gog arranged that we would lunch at the RAF station dining hall. Our normal away from camp lunch was usually a very basic and uninspired pack lunch. This time we hit the jackpot! RAF Lyneham had just moved onto outside catering and the result was something of a showpiece. We had never seen anything like it before as a full scale hot and cold buffet lay waiting for us. The RAF personnel dining looked askance as about sixty of us in denison smocks, sporting face veils like cravats, tore into the repast. The uniformed waitresses even encouraged us to go back for seconds. After lunch we lay on the airstrip, under the shaded protection of the Beverley aircraft wings, sleeping off our gargantuan meal. It was a considerable effort to drag ourselves aboard the plane when the time came for action. Now we understood why our basic Army rations were designed to keep us lean and mean!

On the 18th June we participated in Infantry Tank Training at Bulford in glorious weather.

The outside world seemed to be at relative peace with itself and only two items of real interest caught our attention. Brigitte Bardot the French actress whose pin up picture adorned many a military locker got married to Jacques Charrier and Sweden's Ingemar Johansson wrested the heavyweight Boxing Championship from American Floyd Patterson. The good weather continued into July and we were whisked off to do a parachuting demonstration to a T.A. Brigade in South Wales. 'C' Company were fast making a name for themselves in the world of parachuting demonstrations.

In July a study was released showing that the average male worker in Britain earned £13 2/11d a week and there was much talk, that even all found, we were slipping behind in the earning stakes.

Pay rise or no pay rise, we took part in a Battalion drop on 23rd July at Catterick in Yorkshire called fittingly enough 'Catterick Caper'. This exercise was to have the added attraction of a heavy drop of four rigged platforms after the troop drop had been completed. The platforms contained jeeps and some heavy armaments. We dropped onto the heathery wastes of Catterick moor, and once we landed we had been briefed to rendezvous on the blue smoke. Leading us was Sergeant Joe Murray a fairly aged Para of World War 2 vintage and we set off after him as he led us off the Dropping Zone. On the way Johnny Leaver remarked to me that should we not be heading for the blue smoke? Our leader was heading straight for what was clearly a green smoke canister. I shrugged it off by saying to Johnny that maybe the flare colour had been changed and nobody had thought to tell us, and anyway Joe seemed to be pretty sure of just where he was heading. We plodded on for a time until we spotted another Platoon heading for the same smoke! Sergeant Joe was informed of this and we then realised that he had been taking us to the wrong place for us to rendezvous. Now we had to turn back and retrace our steps towards the far side of the DZ where, by now, the blue flare had died away to a few remaining wisps. Apart from us the DZ was now entirely free of paras as they were all lined up at their planned take off points–free except for us jogging as fast as we could to our appointed place. Halfway across, suddenly Beverleys loomed in the skies and started to spill their loads. Now a heavy drop can be a spectacular sight at the best of times, but when it happens right over your head it is quite a different matter. We had to take sharp avoiding action as the rigged loads floated earthwards under their multiple parachutes. When we caught up with our actual off DZ position our new OC Captain Callaghan was literally jumping with rage and no doubt considerable relief. We then spent a couple of days on company exercise against a Guards Battalion to justify our trip north.

In between this soldiering activities, our social life in Aldershot and district continued as well. The Aldershot Palais was our main dancing venue with outings to Farnborough Town Hall and Camberley. Our watering hole was the Havelock Arms with Les the landlord a very welcoming host. The gantry of his bar was a sight to behold. From it was suspended watches of every description with small labels attached The idea was that when one ran short of funds, you handed your watch over for, say, £2. Les would write your name and unit on the tag and it hung from the gantry until you paid back your dues. Some of the watches dated back to the time of the last war to airborne soldiers who had never returned from active service and therefore would never be reclaimed. It was in a sense a very moving part of Airborne history.

There were other diversions as well. I was approached at one point by a member of 'C' Company whom I shall refer to as Gary. Pay parade was on a Thursday and our weekly wage amounted to £9 2/-a week as a private soldier. Everybody hit Aldershot for the next three nights, so most soldiers were financially strapped by the start of the next week. Gary contacted me early one Saturday morning and requested a £3 loan to enable him to go up to London or 'up smoke' in his parlance. The first time he asked me I made some excuse but on the second occasion I weakened and coughed up the £3. Despite his promise to repay this loan I did not hold out any great hopes. An early morning train ran from London to Farnborough that we called the 'milk-run'. One could alight at Farnborough and then stroll down Queens Avenue to the billet in Albuhera Barracks. Monday morning Gary rolled in at this early hour, and to my surprise, handed me back £5 as we prepared for morning parade. He refused the £2 change, saying blithely that I could consider it interest on the loan. This arrangement continued for quite some time and I found the rate of interest on the advance very rewarding. At times Gary would return very flush with cash and spent it accordingly. I was so content with our arrangement that I thought it impolite to question that aspect. Eventually as they say all good things come to an end–and this was going to be no different.

One Monday morning Gary limped back into the billet of the 'milk-run' train in pretty bad shape. Clearly he had been beaten up very badly with blackened eyes, bruises and cuts to his face, limping badly and with his right arm in an improvised sling. Now Gary was a powerfully built young man with a reputation for looking after himself. We plied him with questions–had he been jumped by a Teddy boy gang or such like? He refused to give us any details and reported sick before parade. A medical examination revealed two cracked ribs and a chipped elbow bone and he was placed on light duties.

That night we managed to get out of him just what had happened. It appears that Gary went up London to indulge in a spot of 'queer-bashing'! London had some pubs such as 'The Standard' and the 'White Bear' that were well known homosexual haunts. Gary would drift in posing as a gay and select a target, preferably one with money and an overseas visitor. The target would eventually take him back to their flat or hotel room. Once there Gary would emerge in his true colours and threaten his gay companion with violence unless he came across with money. This threat was sufficient to put Gary in funds and it was highly unlikely that the target would complain either to the Police or the hotel manager. They would simply put it down to experience, while Gary went off to live the high life in London for the rest of the weekend.

This Saturday, Gary had picked up what he thought was a very refined Canadian professor over here attending some high level conference. They retired to his Park Lane hotel suite with Gary no doubt rubbing his hands at the forthcoming big pay-off. To his surprise the academic turned out to be a martial arts expert and Gary came off second best in the fracas that developed. He admitted to us that it was debatable as to what was the most wrecked in the end–him or the hotel suite!

Needless to say there was no fiver for me this time round. A month or so later Gary, now restored to rude health, had the nerve to touch me for another £3 loan. I had very little difficulty in letting him know that my short-lived career as a banker/pimp had now come to an end.

Early August saw the advent of summer block leave. Six of us made plans to head over to Paris for a few days at the start of the leave period before heading off to our various homes. Passports were organised and everything was set to go. Then the curse of rear party struck me again, and I was the only one of our group detailed to stay on rear party while the main party of the Battalion set off on leave. We were going on leave a few days later but it scuppered my plans of going with the others.

I set off along a week later and hitch hiked to Dover to catch the overnight ferry to Calais. The ferry was jam-packed with noisy French school children returning home. As I stood on the ferry rail, watching as we pulled out of Dover, I became aware of a pretty dark haired girl standing beside me on the crowded deck. We got into conversation and I learned that her name was Doreen Wright from South Shields and that she was heading for a holiday in Majorca. Doreen had just qualified as a teacher and to celebrate she had booked a holiday in Majorca with some student group. She had missed her direct flight from Gatwick airport and had been told to proceed to Paris in the first instance. Once there she had to catch a train to Lyon in the south and then a short flight direct to Palma.

The ferry was so crowded that we sat up all night drinking coffee and chatting until the ferry docked in Calais at dawn.

We shared a train into Paris and found that her train did not leave until that evening. It gave us a day to explore the city together starting with a late breakfast of coffee and croissants in an open air café. We window-shopped along the elegant Rue de Faubourg St Honore, gaped at the Eiffel Tower and strolled along the Champs-Elysees in the warm sunshine. A long lingering lunch washed down with an excellent Chablis was enjoyed in a delightful little restaurant on the Rue St Benoit just off St Germain de Prés. Here we practised our schoolroom French and the young waiters entered into the spirit of things. The afternoon called for a stroll hand in hand along the Seine until the incredibly resonant bells of Notre Dame Cathedral beckoned us. We took photographs of one another on one of the many bridges crossing the Seine near Notre Dame. All too soon it was time for Doreen to catch her train connection to Lyon. She promised to send a postcard from Palma and we made tentative plans to meet up back in the U.K. when our holidays were over. I saw her on her train at 7 p.m. and we kissed goodbye on the Gare de L'Ouest. It was a strange feeling being left alone in Paris after enjoying one another's company for so long.

I booked into a modest hotel and next day wandered round Paris but it was not the same without somebody to talk to and share the event. Late afternoon I was sitting outside a small café enjoying a glass or two of red wine. I observed that several very attractive women seemed to be standing or strolling about as if they were waiting for somebody. Every so often their male companion would turn up and off they would go. I simply thought that this must be a well known Parisian rendezvous. One very pert young girl glanced my way several times as I stared admiringly. She was very shapely and bore a striking resemblance to the French actress

Brigitte Bardot in the way her hair was styled and even down to the way her blouse collar was upturned. It was very warm sitting in the sun and by now the wine had lulled me into a very relaxed frame of mind. I am not sure at what stage during my unabashed ogling that 'Brigitte Bardot' turned and made very direct eye contact with me before mincing over to my table and sitting down. Slightly surprised, but thinking that Christmas had come early, I was about to invite her to join me in a glass of wine. I was even more surprised to learn that I was drinking in a well known red light area and 'Brigitte' was offering me her services in no uncertain manner. Inspired no doubt by the wine and mindful of the Auld Alliance I thought it would be churlish to refuse. I found myself nodding my head in assent. "Venez avec moi!" said 'Brigitte' and taking my hand led me across the street to a block of flats. Once inside we climbed a staircase and on the landing were met by an older woman in a tight costume and a little hat sporting a large feather. The wine was really getting to work on me because this older woman looked exactly like Marlene Dietrich the film actress. She had the same high cheekbones and slightly slanting eyes like the film star and spoke in the same husky voice. The two women conversed in rapid French while I stood silently by. When they had finished 'Brigitte' turned on her heels and went off down the staircase and presumably back to her beat. 'Marlene Dietrich' then conducted me along the corridor and stopped by a door where we were joined by a fat greasy man dressed in vest and trousers and carrying a huge bunch of keys. More talking ensued and by this time my ardour was definitely cooling. I realised that before opening the door the touchy subject of money for the forthcoming services was about to be concluded. A price in francs was mentioned, but it did not register with me as my befuddled brain was by now working overtime looking for a way to get out of this situation. It came to me in a flash. I remained poker faced when the fee was stated and after a moment or two, as if I was considering the price, I said "pour toute la nuite?" The fat pimp looked astonished while 'Marlene Dietrich' who was probably looking forward to a busy night's trade and regarded me as the first notch on her suspender belt, could only gasp "Oh mais non!" her price tariff clearly did not make allowance for a young Scotsman looking for a cheap bed for the night with, no doubt, a full breakfast thrown in!

The deal quickly foundered after this and I was able to stroll off down the corridor. As I descended the stair 'Marlene Dietrich' had sufficiently recovered her composure to scream something at me in French. Whatever words she used were most certainly missing from the French curriculum of Inverness Royal Academy.

Once I gained the sunlit street I could not resist giving a wave to 'Brigitte' who was back at her stance outside the café. She too looked amazed, clearly not used to such a fast operator not realising that she was witnessing a 'virgin soldier' making good his escape. I decided to go easy on the wine from that point onwards. That night I fell in with some French Paras home on leave from their current troubles in Algeria. One of their lot called Phillipe had very good English having studied art for a time in London. I drifted around with them for a couple of days as they did the round of their various relatives and friends. Then I made the decision to head home to Scotland to enjoy the rest of the leave period and bid a fond adieu to Paris.

When I stepped off the train back home in Inverness I selected a postcard to send to Doreen so that it would be waiting for her when she returned home. She had never been in Scotland and had told me her impression was that it was mountainous like Switzerland and always rained. The postcard depicted a shaggy Highland cow with a sun hat draped over its horns and a hot sun beating down from a cloudless sky.

Back home her postcard from Palma already awaited me informing me that she had arrived safely and caught up with the rest of her student group and was enjoying her holiday very much.

After the first week, brother Gerry took a few days holiday due to him and we decided to head for a spot of climbing in Wester Ross. So on Thursday 20th August we took off in Gerry's car and our first port of call was Beauly village to stock up on some provisions. Back in the car Gerry tossed me a copy of that day's Daily Express saying almost conversationally "Looks like a bad air crash." The banner headlines read "32 DIE– HOLIDAY GIRLS ON WAY HOME IN PEAK HORROR!"

I felt a sinking feeling in the pit of my stomach but at first was slightly relieved to see that the crash had occurred in mainland Spain just north of Barcelona. However, as I read on my initial worst fears were realised. The plane, a Dakota, had crashed into the Montesny Mountains some 25 miles north of Barcelona and their were no survivors. The aircraft had been hired by the National Union of Students and was taking students home from holiday in Majorca. Among the passenger list was one Miss D. Wright (British). I was stunned to think that the pretty and vivacious young girl who had been my companion in Paris had come to such a tragic end. What a cruel twist of fate had determined that she had missed her flight going out to Majorca, but had boarded the doomed flight from Barcelona airport. We continued with our climbing break, but I am afraid Gerry did not find me on this occasion the most convivial of companions.

Later that week I got back the developed photographs from the Paris trip and I must confess I found it difficult to look on the picture of a laughing and carefree Doreen on the bridge at Notre Dame.

The French have a word for it 'C'est la vie'–but it did not make it any easier.

CHAPTER 14

NORWAY
EXERCISE 'BAR FROST'

September 1959–February 1960

> Oh we know the way the game is played
> and how we are to win.
> And we curse or laugh and like it
> As we learn to take it on the chin.
>
> Anon.

Returning to Aldershot in late August after my leave I had to take stock as it came as a mild shock to realise that I was now well into my final year of service. As if to remind me, the poster in the theatre agent's window now proclaimed that 'The Mousetrap' was now in its 7th record breaking year. At this rate it might well see out my army service. Back in Albuhera Barracks the Battalion, returned from summer block leave, was looking forward to a hectic year ahead.

The new recruits who had joined us after our return from Cyprus had settled in well. I found much in common with Jim Wilkie who came from Dundee but had attended Aberdeen University for a couple of years. Jim had been suspended for some reason that he never quite made clear to us and most certainly this blot on his career eminently qualified him to join the ranks of 'C' Company. Coming down from University he was immediately liable for National Service and probably thought that joining the Paras was tantamount to enlisting in the Foreign Legion. He was an accomplished violinist with an inability to handle alcohol that was quite touching.

Now Frank Brady from Norwich who came to 'C' Company at the same time had no problem in that department. Frank drank copious amounts of Guinness, seemingly without any effect. Barrel-chested and powerfully built with an engaging chuckle that was like a volcano rumbling, he could be a most entertaining companion for a night out on the town.

Gog was happy with life as 'C' Company, despite its dubious reputation, was heading once again for the title of Champion Company for the second successive year.

In early September Prime Minister Harold Macmillan announced that the General Election would be held on 8th October and Hugh Gaitskell the Labour leader cut short a visit to Moscow commenting "Labour victory is vital for the world."

My 22nd birthday came round on 10th September and was celebrated with fifteen of us going on a mammoth pub crawl round Aldershot which I understand went into 'C' Company folk lore. On September 14th the Russians cracked on with their space programme with a spectacular crashing of Lunik-11 onto the surface of the moon. This was the first man-made object to ever reach our nearest neighbour in space.

1 Para too were soon to be off on their travels as word spread that we were about to take part in an exercise in Norway to be called Exercise 'Bar Frost' along with 3 Para. In mid September the two Battalions were transported to Invergordon in Ross-shire which was practically my home port. Once there we embarked on four ships the Bermuda, Apollo, Saintes and the Camperdown and spent six days at sea cooped up in uncomfortable conditions as we headed towards Scandinavia.

We disembarked on 23rd September at Trondheim. This process occupied the whole of a long boring day as some two thousand Paras got ashore to be trucked to a tented encampment at Vaernes next to the airfield. Here we spent three days and nights in reasonably cold weather. The tented village with fires burning looked for all the world like a large Indian reservation. During our stay Arnhem Day was celebrated with a drum-head service on the airfield attended by HRH The Crown Prince of Norway. On 25th September our CO along with the recce party dropped with 3 Para at a DZ well inside the Arctic Circle. Casualties on our side were minor, but an American contingent had suffered one fatality along with other injuries. That news was broken to us by Sgt 'Buzz-Buzz' Kennedy as he toured our tents late at night doing a roll call. He averred that in his opinion the Yanks used chutes more suited to the gentler climes of Arizona than to the brisker elements encountered in Europe.

Next day was our turn to go. We rose at 5 a.m. on a cold frosty morning and, after a hurried breakfast, marched to the nearby airfield to enplane. We got aboard our Hastings and sat down with our bulky weapon containers. As the aircraft took to the skies leaving Vaernes airfield far behind we settled down on the hard tin seats as best we could to face the long three hour flight ahead.

About half an hour into the flight I was dozing like many others when Jim Hunt nudged me awake. "Hey, Hughie what do you make of that?" He was twisted sideways looking out of one of the small port hole windows. I turned as well to get a proper view and could see the wing of the Hastings quite clearly. A stream of liquid appeared to be streaming over the wing and then whipped away by the slipstream. "I dunno" I mused "maybe it is some de-icing stuff." There was no evidence of rain either. One or two others joined our little discussion group until one of the RAF air dispatchers came to investigate. He paled and dashed off in the direction of the cockpit.

Almost immediately the pilot appeared and announced that something had happened to a fuel stop cock and that the fuel was pouring over the wing. Not only was this creating a fire hazard, but we would have insufficient fuel for the trip, and so we were heading back to Vaernes. We touched down back at the airfield, refuelled and sped off to catch up with the rest of the airborne flotilla.

We learned later that the fuel stop cock had not been secured properly during pre-flight servicing and as a result an RAF ground crew member was court martialled.

Well into our flight by now and having caught up with the other aircraft a certain boredom set in. Two rows of Paras sitting facing each other on hard tin seats running down both sides of the aircraft for a number of hours can get a bit tedious. A bulky main parachute on your back, a reserve on your chest and wearing a Mae West life jacket under our denison smock while cradling a bulky weapon container did not do much to help matters.

Roger Paul decided at some point to enliven things and had assumed the role of Company joker from Cpl Bob 'Punchie' Ash. He requested a sick bag from a passing despatcher. When it was delivered to him naturally all eyes were fixed on him. Roger blew into the bag to expand it and held it in his hand for a while, as he looked suitably fragile. Suddenly he whipped the sick bag to his mouth and bent over making terrible retching sounds. The lines of Paras moved uncomfortably as there was little or no way of avoiding Roger's vomiting performance. At last his retching subsided and he sat back wiping his mouth with the back of his hand. Very deliberately, knowing that all eyes were still on him he carefully swirled the bulky sick bag in his hand and then raised it back to his mouth. Tilting his head he went through the motions of drinking the contents! The effect was traumatic with several Paras now retching in sympathy while others bombarded Roger with anything that came to hand. An air despatcher had to come to restore order, while Roger with a broad grin on his face, burst the empty sick bag to bring the curtain down on his personal floor show.

After what seemed ages we prepared for 'Action Stations' with a certain amount of relief. Standing up in our stick formations, bowed under the weight of the weapon containers, we had an uncomfortable ten minutes as the Hastings descended rocking slightly as it met with air turbulence.

Green light flashed and we were off exiting the aircraft in good style. The sudden transformation from the darkened, stuffy interior of the Hastings into the cold, bright Arctic air was as always a shock to the system. When my chute developed, one is trained to always look up to check that it has developed properly. Once in the Battalion, such niceties like so many others go by the board. Anyway, it did with me on this occasion. I was getting ready to lower my container when I observed something dangling in front of my helmet. It was like a white piece of cord. Now I looked up–and a heart stopping sight greeted me! The rigging lines leading to the parachute periphery were in a sorry state. On one side a number appeared to have snapped and as a result part of the canopy was drooping in a most alarming fashion. It was one of the snapped rigging lines that had draped onto my helmet and alerted me to the condition of my chute. I could also see several rips in the canopy, as if the rigging line situation was not enough to contend with. The rips in the canopy did not bother me too much as I knew the reinforced panels of the chute would contain this. The state of the rigging lines was quite another matter however.

It did not take a degree in physics to work out that if everything stayed as it was I could get down to earth in good shape, but if I lowered the heavy weapon container–what then? The jolt of the container as I lowered it on to the end of the nylon rope might prove too much for the remaining rigging lines to sustain. There would be a very real possibility then that I could part company with the parachute. It was a test that I was unwilling to take part in.

I had carried the reserve chute on my chest for so many jumps that it was now time to see what it was made of. I yanked on the red handle. The canvas container fell apart and the white chute spilled out lazily. I shook it like somebody removing crumbs from a teacloth, and it slowly filled with air and drifted upwards somewhat smaller than my main chute but nonetheless a welcoming sight. Now that I adjudged there was sufficient parachute support above me I turned my attention to lowering the weapon container as Norway, in the shape of the DZ, was not that far away. My troubles were not over. To my alarm the reserve chute started to wrap round the main chute, hampering its full development. If I used my hands to steer it clear of the main chute, I would not be able to lower the container still attached to me with all the dire consequences that that would entail. Necessity is the mother of invention. I brought up my right boot to face level, and used it to force the reserve chute away from its death wish of wrapping itself round the main chute. This worked beautifully and I was able, despite my ballet like position, to successfully lower the container. Disaster struck when I tried to regain a normal parachuting position and use my hands on the wayward reserve chute. My foot slipped and the lift web of the reserve chute wrapped itself round my ankle and jerked it upwards with considerable force. The reserve chute now billowed gracefully above me and there was no physical way I could twist my body to release the lift web. It was as if my foot was caught in a vice. I was by now hanging the wrong way up, literally strung up by the feet. Below me the DZ was alarmingly close and I was oscillating wildly as I had no means of controlling the parachute. I was aware of the countryside blurring and the thought did occur to me that perhaps the blood rushing to my head was affecting my vision. There was little I could do but shut my eyes and grit my teeth as I prepared to head-butt Norway.

To my total surprise, and overwhelming relief, my fall was broken by some small stunted trees and tussocky heather. I lay there for a minute or two, giving due thanks for my deliverance, in much the same way as I had done after my first Battalion jump in Cyprus. As I was gathering my wits and preparing to undo my weapon container I became aware of a Norwegian officer in a large grey great coat striding towards me. He was clearly a DZ officer in charge of proceedings on the ground and was possibly bracing himself for the worst. He viewed me unwrapping my container in open mouthed silence. I suspect that he either had no English or was totally unprepared for the sight of a latter-day Lazarus rising from the Arctic wastes. About a score of other 1 Para jumpers experienced similar type problems with their chutes. We were told at a later date that an enquiry found that the chutes had been stored in an unheated hanger overnight and a sharp frost had affected some chutes stored at one exposed end. The top story belong to Johnny Grant (no relation) from the Intelligence Section whose mains static line had snapped on leaving the aircraft. He struck a developed chute off somebody who had jumped before him, and this temporary arrestment of his downward plunge gave him enough time to pull his reserve and land safely.

Johnny thus qualified for the 'Caterpillar Club' which is reserved for those whose life has been saved by direct use of a reserve parachute.

Technically I did not qualify, as my main chute was still functioning, but I know within myself that my reserve chute certainly saved my bacon on this particular occasion!

By now 1 Para were littered all over the DZ, collecting their gear from the weapon containers and stumbling through the knee high heather to the various rendezvous points indicated by coloured smoke flares. When I flopped down with the rest of the assembling 'C' Company personnel Gog doing a head count greeted me, not with open arms but with the passing comment, "Hey Grant, what kind of f****ing acrobatics were you up to, up there. You were like a bloody Christmas turkey hanging up in a butcher's shop!" I just smiled weakly in return, only too happy to be reclining safe and sound in the Arctic heather.

We moved out shortly afterwards to play at soldiers.

We were to fight against a Norwegian brigade who were supposed to oppose our arrival and further movements once we had landed. Our task was to capture and secure nearby Bardufoss airfield. To this end on the night of 26th and 27th we carried out a night advance up Andsfjell, a mountain over 2000 feet high and at dawn carry out a flanking attack on the defending Norwegian forces. The Norwegians had decided that the mountain approach was safe especially at night and with very difficult terrain. Of course this was right up our CO's street so up and over the hill we went. To say that it was difficult was an understatement and having to ford several rushing streams full of icy cold water. Our only consolation was that as long as we were moving it kept hypothermia at bay in the frosty conditions. Once over the hill we continued our advance against the startled Norwegians until later that day poised to take Bardufoss airfield the Exercise was concluded. At last we were able to get some 'scoff' (food) and a few hours sleep. We returned to Aldershot on 3rd October and a well earned 48 hour pass.

The following week was spent in Aldershot before we left for Exercise 'Red Banner', the 3rd Division mobility exercise held on Salisbury Plain. The 'enemy' this time were to be 1st Guards Brigade. A successful drop was carried out on the Imber DZ. Successful that is for all save the hapless 'Gungy' Gordon! 'Gungy' had boarded the aircraft with a considerable hangover and declared his intention of going sick once the jump was concluded. The idea of playing soldiers against the Guards for some four days exposed to the elements and without a 'hair of the dog' was not appealing to him. Now it was common knowledge that if you said you had a bad back after a jump it was almost impossible for any suspicious Sergeant Major to deny it. So a bad back was what 'Gungy' was going to have. Once we landed I was jogging clutching all my gear along with two or three others as we headed towards our Company rendezvous point. We came across 'Gungy' lying groaning very realistically beside his now collapsed chute clearly waiting for a DZ medic to stumble over him.

"They should give 'Gungy' a bloody Oscar for that performance!" commented Frank Brady to our group as we skirted his body and pressed onwards. That night as we bedded down under the stars word filtered through to us that 'Gungy' was a very real casualty. Apparently in landing he had picked a spot where some past exercise had left a shallow trench and in encountering this had fallen awkwardly and broken some small bone in his back! As the old 'C' Company saying goes 'Those who pray to the gods shall have their mess tin filled to over-flowing!'

'Red Banner' ended some four days later when we pursued the Guards to Sidbury Hill where the final attack was launched.

Returning to Aldershot and civilisation we heard that Prime Minister Harold Macmillan had won the election with a thumping majority.

October ended with the Battalion Rifle meeting which was won by 'C' Company much aided by our two Company crack shots Cpls Jim Hunt and 'Mitch' Mitchell.

This month saw the death at 50 years of age of Errol Flynn the hell-raising Hollywood swashbuckler as well as that of the tenor Mario Lanza.

After the activities of the past few months, November was mainly Aldershot based and reasonably humdrum. Two new Platoon officers joined us at this time Lt Emms and Lt Penley. Lt 'Rudge' Penley is worthy of mention. The son of an Admiral he had won the Sword of Honour at Sandhurst and became the first officer to be ever directly commissioned into the Parachute Regiment. Before 'Rudge', officers volunteered from other regiments, and had to undergo 'P' Course before being accepted.

Tall and with a thatch of reddish hair Rudge quickly became accepted and respected by the 'Toms' of 'C' Company.

December was rounded off with a Company exercise in Jersey which was much enjoyed by one and all. During our stay we were honoured by a visit from the Governor, General Sir George W.E. Erskine K.CB.K.B.E. D.S.O.

In mid December our old friend Archbishop Makarios was elected first President of the new Republic of Cyprus. As thousands of Cypriots gathered to celebrate in Metaxas Square, Makarios in his address paid tribute to "the heroes and martyrs" of the recent liberation struggle.

The teenage musical movement started in the fifties, was by now well established with the emergence of a British singer to rival Elvis Presley, called Cliff Richard.

We proceeded on block Christmas leave and I travelled north with George Brown. I broke my journey to spend a couple of days in his home town of Biggar before heading home for Inverness.

Celebrating Hogmanay back home in Inverness it was a sobering thought (well almost!) to realise that I was not only entering a new decade, but the end of my national service. Christmas leave soon passed and early January saw some notable gaps in our ranks. Cpls Jim Hunt and 'Jake' Jacobs along with Ptes Surtees, Duffy, Gaskin and Hancox went off to sample the rigours of civilian life. So many of our old faces from the Cyprus days were fading away.

In January for the want of something better to do, Gog dreamed up the idea of Initiative Tests. This took the form of leaving Aldershot in two man teams to track down a variety of pre-determined tasks. Some tasks were run of the mill but others had a more glamorous side to them like locating such well-known personalities as Professor Jimmy Edwards, Norman Wisdom, Dr Barbara Moore the marathon walker and the Governor of Her Majesty's Prison Dartmoor. Ptes Davison and Boswarva who drew the latter task were asked by Gog to convey festive greetings to any former 'C' Company members they ran into during their visit. We were allowed to swap places in the teams so that compatible characters teamed up. George Brown joined me and our task was to obtain the signature of Norman Wisdom who was appearing in Pantomime in Manchester.

We were not allowed to take any money with us and were actually body searched to this end before we set off. We hitchhiked up to Birmingham and reached Wolverhampton as darkness was falling along with a heavy snowfall. If there was ever a time when I decided that my military career would finish with the end of my three year engagement–then this was it! Tired, cold and hungry I saw young office workers meeting up to go for a drink and prepare for a weekend's enjoyable activity and not for the first time I realised that there was another life after the Army.

Earlier that month I had passed an NCO's cadre and been promoted to L/Cpl. This was par for the course as I was on the run in to my demob in early summer. Needless to say on this occasion I did not bother to send Gerry a postcard!

On the outskirts of Wolverhampton we were given a lift by a lorry driver. Just our luck–he was bound for his home in Manchester and would take us all the way there. He had also done his National Service some years before so he had a strong sense of fellow feeling towards us. He informed us that we could spend the night at his house, and after a meal and wash up, he would even drive us to the theatre that Norman Wisdom was appearing in. This all sounded highly civilised to George and myself.

Nearing Manchester he divulged to us that he and his wife were in the process of divorcing,and with no family to complicate the situation, were still sharing the same roof. Arriving at his house and after parking the lorry we all entered the house. His wife, who he told us worked in a local factory, was in the lounge smoking with her hair in curlers looked at us in mild surprise. Instead of introducing us Alfie, our lorry driver friend, busied himself with writing a long note which he handed to his wife. She read it at length and then penned back a reply to him on the same note. We realised then that the couple might well be living under the same roof but relations had clearly got to the stage when they were not speaking to each other. Communication was strictly by written notes. Introduction clearly having been done, his wife departed to get herself ready for a date that same evening while Alfie knocked up some food for the three of us in the kitchen. He embarrassed us by saying that we could have his bed upstairs and that he would sleep in the lounge in a bed settee. We protested, but Alfie regarded us as house guests and would have none of it.

There was a humorous side to this troubled household. During our meal, some point of discussion arose and Alfie said that he would, in his words, 'ask the wife' and proceeded to write her another note! George and I found it hard not to laugh. After our repast Alfie was as good as his word and drove us to the theatre in down town Manchester. As it was getting near curtain time we could not get access to Norman Wisdom, but a helpful commissionaire obtained a signed photograph of Norman so that we had tangible proof that we had completed our task. Alfie then took us to his social club where a night of some serious drinking took place and it did not cost us a penny.

Returning to the house at some ungodly hour a further shock was in store for us when he showed us to his bedroom. From our talk in the cab and elsewhere we had gathered that he was a fairly committed Manchester United supporter, but we did not suspect that he was a fanatic. His bedroom was awash with photographs of the late Busby Babe team all suitably draped in black! A large picture of Duncan Edwards dominated the room, making the shrine to the team complete. It was an eerie feeling waking up in the morning, as if one had fallen asleep during a memorial service.

Alfie saw that we had a good breakfast in the morning, between exchanging a flurry of written notes with his estranged spouse, and drove us to the outskirts of Manchester to see us safely on our way back to Aldershot.

January ended with a young unknown Senator John F. Kennedy from Massachusetts tossing his hat into the ring of Presidential hopefuls. He was considered a long shot due to his relative inexperience and the fact that he was a Catholic.

Not long after our return to Aldershot, George Brown was promoted to Sergeant and posted to Airborne Forces Depot to assist in the basic training and selection of the next generation of recruits hoping to join the Parachute Regiment.

"The wind of change is blowing through this continent.........." thus said Prime Minister Macmillan when addressing the South African Parliament in Capetown in early February. 'C' Company experienced its own wind of change when we moved to Sennybridge in heavy snow falls and drifting snow with commendable fortitude. We also experienced the hazards of live firing with section and Platoon fire and movement while rediscovering the limitations of a Company's fire power. The infallibility of the compass was re-learned. From Sennybridge we moved on to the equally harsh climes of Brecon. Here ensued a rigorous patrols exercise with individual map reading and compass work being the dominant theme. Anti ambush drill took a high priority with the few remaining old sweats from the Cyprus days passing on the benefit of our hard earned experience to the greener members of the company.

The highlight of our training session in Wales was a day spent on the grenade range at Sennybridge with Lt Penley in charge. It was a day of hard frost with a cold biting wind adding to the general discomfort of things. Priming grenades became something of a game of Russian roulette as frozen hands struggled to put the components of the grenade together. One or two grenades that did not explode after being thrown made 'Rudge' Penley wisely decide to call it a day. To celebrate the end of our training stint in Wales it was decided to have a Company night out at a pub in Brecon using a 'kitty' from company funds.

Lt Penley was of a mind to come with us and gently supervise events. Wiser counsels prevailed, as 'C' Company letting their hair down was not an edifying sight at the best of times, and nothing that he had been taught at Sandhurst would be of any service to him in what could be a traumatic new experience. As Sgt 'Nobby' Arnold said to him "Best be around next day, Sir–to pick up the pieces!"

We returned to the gentler climes of Aldershot towards the end of February. I prepared to pick up the ropes again in the company office, when Gog stalked in and throwing down his pace stick addressed me. "Right-ho Grant–I've got a secret mission for you to do!"

CHAPTER 15

THE END OF THE ROAD

March 1960–June 1960

"Keep right on to the end of the road,
Keep right on round the bend".

Harry Lauder song.

Gog's secret mission was soon revealed to me in all its detail. A craze for marathon walking had swept the country with the redoubtable Dr Barbara Moore courting massive publicity as she walked from John O' Groats to Lands End. Such was the public interest in this event that Billy Butlin himself jumped on the band wagon. Billy Butlin was a flamboyant showman whose holiday camps were very popular with a public slowly recovering from the austerity of wartime Britain. Butlin quickly organised a much publicised John O' Groats to Lands End walk with excellent cash prizes as an inducement. The public were invited to apply and apply they did in their thousands. The walk was to commence on Friday 26th February and by that time well over 5,000 applications had been received.

Billy Butlin and his wife flew up to Wick airport and then by car to the starting point at John O' Groats. There he fired a flare before the massed media to start the race. Some 1,500 actually started the walk, and soon many fell by the wayside. The Royal Northern Infirmary at Inverness was inundated with walkers asking for treatment for blistered feet and some twenty six people had to seek national assistance to get back home. The ones with more stamina and better organisation carried on with the long trek to the south.

Gog explained to me that our Regimental interest derived from the fact that two ex-Paras from the White City TA unit were taking part. Their names were CSM Butler and 'Tex' Banwell. It was decided to wait and see how the race progressed before a decision was made to provide some form of back up service to our two walkers. Gog asked me to stand by and on no account to tell anybody what was afoot–in a manner of speaking!

A week or so passed and the whole nation appeared to be avidly following the daily fortunes of the assorted walkers. The general field had thinned considerably as the walkers crossed the Scottish border. Some of the walkers were almost professionally supported by back up teams and our two chaps began to feel the strain in competing against them. It was time for me to be sprung into action!

Gog instructed me to take a jeep with a cook/driver and proceed with all haste to the White City TA in London for further instructions. I threw a few items together and disappeared from the billet leaving an unexplained empty bed space.

'Chuck' Parsons was the appointed driver/cook and we reported to the White City later in the morning. A small trailer full of Army 'compo' rations complete with mobile cooking range all covered with a tarpaulin was hitched on to the jeep. We then set off north to make contact with our walking team.

Contact was made with them at Kidderminster in a school room where the weary walkers had bedded down for the night. Tex was very surprised to be introduced to his new back up team when I roused him from his sleeping bag. It was explained to him that White City were of the opinion that the services of a back up team would help him to compete on a more equal basis with the other front runners. After all the honour of the Regiment had to be thought about. Tex was by now on his own as CSM Butler had fallen out with a torn tendon in his leg.

Before he returned to his sleeping bag we had worked out a plan of campaign for the morrow. Basically I would walk with Tex to give him moral support while Chuck would drive ahead to the planned end of the day's walk to prepare an evening meal and bivouac area. Next day Tex and I walked as far as Worcester and, being relatively fresh, I was able to pull him along at a fair old pace. The other bonus when we reached the end of the day's hike was to find that Chuck had used his airborne initiative in a most commendable way. He would approach a likely looking house and request permission to use their back garden to prepare a meal for his two walkers. Such was the ongoing national interest in Butlin's trek that the householder would insist that we dine with the family and threw in hot baths as well. If any householder did not come across with the goods Chuck simply moved on to find another soft target. Chuck used this ploy all down the line so never once was the mobile range ever put into action. Next day it was off for Gloucester and then to Bristol. Tex seemed to have found his second wind and for my part this walking holiday through rural England was very acceptable. I found Keith Demer 'Tex' Banwell a fascinating character and learned a lot about him as we chatted away during our daily stroll. Before World War 2 he had joined the Coldstream Guards then the Royal Hampshire Regiment and saw service in India, Palestine and Egypt where he taught physical training to the Foreign Legion. During the war he was captured at Tobruk but managed to escape in a stolen vehicle. Taken prisoner for a second time in Crete he was put into a prisoner of war camp. Extremely fit he would box with the German guards one of them being Max Schmelling, the 1930's world heavyweight champion now serving in the German Wehrmacht.

Banwell and another prisoner escaped by stealing a landing craft which ran out of fuel and drifted for nine days before reaching the North African coast.

Here he was hospitalised for three months until his military career took on a strange twist. Somebody noticed that he bore a very striking resemblance to Field Marshal Montgomery who had just led the British forces to victory in North Africa. Tex was sent to Cairo and was driven around in the Field Marshal's staff car so as to confuse any enemy agents. Being a bit taller than the Field Marshal he was under strict orders never to leave the staff, but just be seen driven around.

A return to normal soldiering saw Tex join the Parachute Regiment just in time to take part in the ill-fated drop at Arnhem in September 1944. Taken prisoner for the third time, he once more escaped by jumping from a moving train as it entered Germany and made himself useful by joining the Dutch Resistance movement. Betrayed towards the end of the war he was placed in Auschwitz but not for long as the camp was liberated by the advancing Russian forces and he was able to link up with a British paratroop unit. Understandably Tex was a legendary airborne figure who had complete faith in his own ability to get the best out of any given situation. I was to see examples of this in the days that lay ahead of us.

The days flew by–and so did Bridgwater–Taunton and then on to Exeter. We were making good headway and were well up with the leaders when we became aware that underhand tactics were coming in to play. Certain walkers who were behind us as we started a day's walk would be waiting for us at the end of the allotted span for that day. We knew that they had not passed us at any stage during the day and the fact that they looked remarkably fresh merely confirmed our suspicions.

Clearly they were getting lifts in some way and then strolling into the end of day control point as if they had walked the route. Once deception was rumbled when two walkers who looked and dressed alike were detected as they shared the walking making it look as if only one walker was involved.

We decided to fight fire with fire especially as we were due to cover the long inhospitable stretches of Okehampton and Bodmin moor. Once well into the walk we would find Chuck waiting with the jeep in some isolated lay-by. We would turf out some of the rations to make a cavity in the trailer into which Tex could snuggle and then lash down and secure the tarpaulin cover. We then drove through the lashing rain to a few miles short of the day's control point, wait for a suitable interval and then Tex and I would stroll into the finish in the manner born. In this way we were able to maintain contact with the leading group and cheating was so rife it was virtually the order of the day! The publicity and cash prizes waiting the winners at Lands End was bringing out the best and worst in the competitors.

One lunchtime as Tex and I were on the outskirts of Redruth and heading for Penzance a TV crew cornered us and asked if we would be willing to take part in a highlight to be shown on national TV that night. Naturally we agreed and they waited until a gold coloured Rolls Royce cruised into view and out of it alighted Billy Butlin himself. With the race coming to a thrilling conclusion he was milking the publicity good style and a shot of him with two Paras would make for good viewing. He looked the part of the archetypal millionaire dressed in a light tan overcoat, the collar trimmed with some dark fur and clutching a small torpedo of a cigar. His round florid face, with neatly trimmed moustache, beamed goodwill at one and all as he shook hands with us before walking for about a hundred yards or so in our company until the cameras were satisfied. Then with a hasty aside to us "That's enough f****ing walking for me, boys!" he shot back into his Rolls and departed for Lands End and more camera coverage with a cheery wave of his cigar. Tex and I followed him into Lands End and a day or so later, for Tex to find that he had finished an acceptable sixth and had won £200 was even more acceptable.

Tex spent the day in the Lands End hotel relaxing after his marathon and we decided to wait that night for the arrival home of the first lady competitor Wendy Lewis from Liverpool. Tex did some sort of deal with a sharp suited individual that involved us in doing some publicity work for Coca-Cola. It was good money as we were paid £10 each up front although Tex was not forthcoming about what gross fee he had negotiated. A large crowd had assembled about midnight to greet Wendy as she clocked in with TV arc lights glaring and the national press pack in attendance. In uniform we were able to get to the front and our publicity job was to unveil a small hand held banner in vivid colours that read 'COCA COLA IS THE BEST!' so that the various TV cameras could pick it up as well as the press pack. It was easy money to us mercenaries and we duly obliged. That night we left Lands End to go to an extended house party in the nearby village of Mousehole with some of Tex's newly found admirers. A party that went on all of the next day and the following night that taxed our stamina as much as the walk had done.

Eventually we left by jeep to make it back for the White City base. Nearing Salisbury, Tex decided that it just would not look right if we returned with full rations and an unused mobile range and he knew of a source that would assist us with this problem. This source turned out to be an ex-Para pal of his who now ran a one-man catering enterprise supplying snacks and hot food to the various Army units that used the shooting ranges around Salisbury. The rations were duly exchanged for £60 with Chuck and I receiving our cut of £10 apiece while Tex as usual enjoyed the lion's share. We were starting to find that following Tex about was quite rewarding in its own way. Flush with money, it was decided to have a night out in Salisbury town to round off our trip and after a slap up meal and a night's carousing in the 'Prince of Wales' pub it was time for Tex to pull his last trick. He decided that we had had enough of roughing it and approached a military Police base and explained to them who we were, and what we had been doing. The end result was that we all three bedded down in relative comfort in the station cells for that night as overnight guests.

By this time I knew Gog could well be sending out search parties or getting ready to charge me with desertion, so we pressed on for the White City to return the now empty trailer. The White City people seemed very pleased with a job well done and asked no awkward questions. Our last task was to deliver Tex back into the bosom of his family somewhere in the East End before heading for Aldershot. When we drove into Tex's street our first impression was that they had left up the Coronation decorations as bunting and flags flew everywhere. Tex's exploits had made him something of a local celebrity and his neighbours were not shy about showing their pride in their charismatic fellow resident.

Another 'knees up' party broke out and Chuck and I found ourselves spending another night in very convivial company so that it was midday next day when we rolled back into Aldershot. Fortunately Gog was out of barracks so I did not have to explain the lengthy delay in our return.

My intention had been on my return to barracks to keep everybody guessing as to what secret mission I had been on–but my cover was blown! When I had slipped away leaving an empty bed-space there was considerable talk in the billet as to what had happened and Gog was tight lipped on the subject. On night as they were viewing supper time TV there was Tex, myself and Billy Butlin walking through Redruth gracefully acknowledging the throngs of spectators.

So it was back to normal business, and the end of March saw 'C' Company taking part in an exercise in North Devon. We were unloaded somewhere in the countryside and had to make our way through 'enemy held' territory to a remote beach. The enemy on this occasion was to be the Devonshire Constabulary assisted by a local TA unit. During our Company briefing one of our Platoon officers remarked that dodging the Police would come as second nature to many of our Company. Our task was to get as many as possible back undetected to the beach for a rendezvous at 7 a.m. We were to travel across country in pairs, covering a distance of some 35 miles. Once on the beach a couple of D.U.K.W.'s would pick us up and ferry us across a wide estuary to a TA base and from there we would be trucked back to Aldershot.

I was teamed up with a newly arrived private called Marlow who had yet to be broken into the 'C' Company mould and even worse harboured a desire to be a career soldier! I knew instinctively that he would not make for the most ideal of travelling companions. We set off across country by compass and made good time until a considerable amount of Police activity forced us to lie up for a while. When I considered it had abated I left Marlow in our hide to go and have a recce as evening was closing in. I walked round a corner of a small country lane and found myself beside a small cottage with a workman loading up a small grey pick-up van. It turned out that he was going to do a job in a village just beyond our pick up point on the beach and was quite agreeable to giving us a lift. This was too good an opportunity to miss, so summoning Marlow we got into the back of the pick-up and the door was closed. Marlow was most unhappy about this bending of the rules and I tried to convince him, without much success, that all is fair in love and war–not forgetting pointless Company exercises! W e passed one or two Police road checks en route but remained undetected crouched down on an uncomfortable bed of cables and sundry tools in the back of our transport. Our temporary chauffeur dropped us off at a point that he reckoned was about three miles away from our beach. Left to our own devices I now had another problem to face. We could stroll on to the beach and linger about there for the rest of the night until our rendezvous time at 7 a.m., or hang about where we had been dropped off. Not to help matters the weather had turned foul with sleety rain and a cold biting wind. No problem to keep warm if you were walking, but pretty miserable just sitting around. In a field close by were several large stacks and I said to Marlow that we could shelter there until time came to make the final dash for the beach.

Marlow, whose confidence in me was now severely dented, elected to move on and hang about close to the beach. So we parted company.

Entering the field I scaled up the stack and, pushing aside some hay near the top, I created a sort of nest into which I snuggled. Lying there out of the biting wind and under the canopy of the stars I was soon lulled into a deep sleep. It was the sound of a tractor close by that awakened me with a start. I realised that it was much brighter than it should have been and a sinking feeling in my stomach confirmed the fact that I had slept in!

The tractor was manned by two farm workers who had come to haul in some fodder from the stack for their livestock. It was a considerable surprise for them when I erupted from the stack before their startled eyes rather like a dancing girl jumping out of a surprise birthday cake! Clambering down the stack, I checked the time with them before haring away across the field in a vain attempt to make the beach in time, leaving them scratching their heads.

Needless to say, when I reached the beach it was empty and tell tale tracks in the sand showing me only too clearly that the D.U.K.W.'s had gone and with them the rest of 'C' Company. They clearly knew that I was missing because some wag had left a big arrow mark gouged in the sand and the words 'ALDERSHOT–THIS WAY!' beside it. I detected the hand of Jim Wilkie had been at work.

I was now faced with a long hike round the estuary to the base on the other side. Naturally when I finally reached it the trucks had already left some time ago for Aldershot. Gog had left a message for me with the chap in charge of the camp to the effect that if I turned up to make my own way back to Aldershot, but if my body was washed up on the estuary–not to bother contacting him!

A long hitch hike back across country to Aldershot was now my lot and when I arrived back I found that some wit had posted an obituary to me on the Company notice board entitled 'Lost in Action–23525694–L/Cpl Grant– Next of Kin have expressly advised that they do not want to be informed!'

The annual Devizes–Westminster Canoe race took place at Easter and 1 Para entered six crews together with 125 others including two from the 3rd Battalion (3 Para) and six from S.A.S. I was invited to make up a team with L/Cpl Davison but declined as I had accepted an invitation to see Paddy and Maree in Manchester during Easter Block leave so Pte Carty took my place.

The race is 125 miles long with 77 locks which have to be portaged and depended greatly on catching the high tide at Teddington to complete the final 15 miles to Westminster. I was not too unhappy to miss out on the watery marathon. Prominent among the teams taking part were a team from 2 Para featuring a certain Captain John Ridgway and Cpl Chay Blyth.

Just before we broke for Easter leave another batch of faces departed our ranks for civvy street–Cpls Roy Boden and Woods along with Ptes Paul, Duffy, Peevor and Wren. The weekend before they left I went for a drink and a game of darts with Roger Paul and 'Jenny' Wren. They were full of what they would do once they had left the army and Jenny confided in me that he was heading along with two pals from 2 Para to be highly paid mercenaries in one of the newly emerged African states that would make use of their services. In two months time or so my own time would be up and I would have to give serious thought as to my own future.

Just before Easter we were back in bleak Dartmoor on Exercise 'Black Knight' and yet another spot of evading a friendly enemy in very unpleasant conditions. Ptes Dobie and Brogan were having troubles of their own and subsequently resisting a very realistic interrogation session.

Easter leave thus came as a welcome break. On the way back I stopped off for an overnight stopover with Paddy and Maree Tomkins in their flat in Manchester's Moss-side now complete with their first born, Brian. Paddy was now working as an assistant cinema manager but still eager to know all about 'C' Company activities.

Back from Easter leave in early April road runs became the order of the day coupled with long tedious days on the firing range. The only thing to enliven this routine was a large Church parade and all us Catholics were told to parade elsewhere. We soon found out what elsewhere was all about. A helicopter awaited us on nearby Frensham Common and we left footers were to assist with certain trials that they wanted to carry out. We were taken aloft six at a time and parachuted out at various heights. It was quite an experience. When summoned to the open door by the despatcher we had to shuffle forward on our bottom until we were sitting on the door sill, our legs dangling into space, looking down on the distant Common, with Frensham pond glinting in the watery sunlight. I was the third person called on to jump so I was able to witness No 2's attempt to exit the chopper. His departure was marred by the fact that his main parachute pack caught the sill of the doorway forcing him into a graceful downwards somersault that is most certainly not recommended practise. The despatcher craned forward anxiously to ensure that he was O.K. then summoned me forward with the shouted words "Don't be like that silly bugger–really push off when you go!" As if he needed to tell me. The drop was longer than usual as the down blast from the rotor blades had a delaying effect on the chute opening. A second drop from a different height, this time sporting a reasonably light weapon container, added two helicopter descents to our Parachute Descent records.

On 22nd April another Exercise loomed up. It would turn out to be my last airborne Exercise with the Regiment and appropriately enough it was called Exercise 'Highland Fling'! even better it was to be held on my very own stamping ground of the Cairngorm Mountains. It was my 37th and final Parachute drop and proved to be text book stuff. We then had to tab (march) some 75 miles in 72 hours across rugged country to Aviemore. We travelled by Kirriemuir–Glen Cova–Glen Callater–Linn of Dee–Larig Ghru whilst conducting side shows with Platoon and Company attacks along with some night patrolling thrown in for good measure.

We Scots in the Battalion had to take some stick as we soldiered our way in atrocious weather across the unforgiving heights of the Cairngorms. Near the Linn of Dee some hill walker, with a nationalistic bent, had written in white paint on a large rock 'GIVE US OUR INDEPENDENCE!' The comments on this by our mainly English comrades in arms were unrepeatable.

Reaching Aviemore, we were entrained back to Aldershot as May and my last complete month in the Army was ushered in.

On 8th May Princess Margaret and Tony Armstrong-Jones were married in Westminster Abbey. The weekend after the big wedding a group of us were sitting in a pub just off Leicester Square and a discussion arose as to Winston Churchill's claim to be the greatest living Englishman. Frank Brady it was who said that it would be little short of a disgrace if we ever had to tell our grandchildren that we had lived in the same period as the great man and had never made the effort to see him. One of our group Steve Bosley said that he knew exactly where Churchill lived in the city and it was not that far away. That settled it and so off we went to pay our respects to the great man in person. We arrived at an imposing house that Bosley confirmed was Churchill's town residence with a lone policeman stationed outside. He viewed us with understandable suspicion when we told him what we were about. Sir Winston was at present out of the country he informed us but if we cared to leave a message he would see that it was delivered to him on his return. A loyal message was hastily written out on a page torn from the Police notebook and we left satisfied with our effort.

Back in the Company office Lt Rudge Penley tried to wind me up by declaring that demob for all Paras had been suspended forthwith due to international sabre rattling by Kruschev the Russian leader. An American U-2 aircraft had violated Russian air space and been shot down with the pilot 30 year old Francis Gary Powers being made a prisoner. The Russians were convinced that the plane had been on a spying mission while the Americans maintained that it was simply carrying out weather research and had strayed off course.

A Conference of the Big Four–Eisenhower, Kruschev, Macmillan and De Gaulle, due to be held in Paris, fell apart in a welter of bitter recriminations and diplomatic farce as a result.

May 18th I sat in the TV lounge with Jim Wilkie and some other Scots watching the majestic Real Madrid football team play Eintracht Frankfurt in the European Cup at Hampden Park.

Real gave a superlative display of attacking football before an enthralled crowd of 130,000 appreciative Scots and goals from Di Stefano (3) and Ferenc Puskas, the Galloping Hungarian Major, (4) emphatically drove home their superiority.

My last major activity on the military front took place with Battalion field firing at Catterick between 21st and 25th May.

We came alarmingly close to reality in the minor tactics; once or twice we advanced through the smoke and assaulted the 'enemy' with bullet and bayonet encroaching to within a few yards of our own supporting fire. Under the auspices of Major Jones, U.S. Army and the combat hardened French officer, we were flattered by the least amount of criticism (at section level) and duly reckoned the most likely to have succeeded.

So on Friday 27th May it was back to Aldershot from the wilds of Yorkshire and into the Havelock Arms to reclaim my wrist watch from Landlord Les for the last time. A deeply emotional moment!

Friday June 10th was my demob date and with nothing major on our soldiering calendar it was a case of handing over the reins of the company office to a new incumbent much as 'Geordie' Rice had done to me in Cyprus many months ago. I gave him much the same advice as I had been given.

As the days to do dwindled events moved quite quickly. On Wednesday 8th June I handed in all my army gear to the Q.M.'s stores–all save my red beret which I had decided to retain as a souvenir. After all it had been gained at some personal cost and discomfort so I was not going to give it up easily. The Stores were quite used to having red berets going missing and 6/11d was deducted from my final pay to reimburse Her Majesty's Forces. Thursday night was a reasonably subdued party in the Havelock Arms–more of a wake as this was to be a parting of the ways.

The final day Friday 10th June. Gog shook my hand matter-of-factly in the office and wished me all the best for civvy street as did Rudge Penley. My red Certificate of Service booklet was signed in my presence by Lt G.D. Emms. I was now effectively discharged and free go to.

I went back down the very same route that I had walked up some three years before. Suitcase in hand, I strode down Hospital Hill, past the cinema and Naafi club and a last look at the theatre agency window to check that 'The Mousetrap' was now in its 8th Great Year and still going strong. So it too had seen out my army service. At the station the taxi drivers were still there patiently waiting for business and sheltering from the rain in their cars.

Boarding the train I sat quietly until the repeated slamming of carriage doors and then a sharp whistle blast signalled the train pulling out of the station for London. And so I took my final leave of Aldershot without a backward look.

Another train–another day.

The London to Inverness train was slowly making its way over the Slochd Summit just south of Inverness and in another half hour or so I would be back in my home town. I pulled out the red Certificate of Service book that Lt Emms had signed to read again. My Military conduct was classified as 'Very Good' which was highly commendable for any 'C' Company graduate. The Testimonial read "Well above average in intelligence Grant has proved himself to be a very good NCO with a well developed sense of duty and loyalty to his Regiment. He is sober minded, conscientious and thoroughly trustworthy and has considerable personal initiative. I have no hesitation in recommending him to any employer." Well, that about said it all then. Three years summed up in half a dozen lines. The train was now breasting the high ground above Culloden Battlefield and down below me stretched that panorama of hills and sea that I knew so well. The mist covered purplish hills to the west and in the foreground the blue waters of the Moray Firth. Down there nestling at the head of the Firth lay Inverness and home–and in a very real sense the rest of my life.

1

(This page to be entirely free from erasure)

Description of Soldier on leaving Army Service

Year of Birth..... *1937*..... Height..... *5*..... ft..... *11½*..... ins.

Complexion..... *FRESH*..... Eyes..... *HAZEL*..... Hair..... *BROWN*.....

Marks and Scars (Visible).....

Assessments of Military Conduct and Character
(To be completed personally by the Commanding Officer)

Military Conduct..... *Very Good*.....

Note—The Range of Military Conduct Gradings possible is:—
    (1) Exemplary (available only to men with a minimum of 6 years' service)
    (2) Very Good (3) Good (4) Fair (5) Indifferent (6) Bad (7) Very Bad

Testimonial. (To be completed with a view to civil employment)

Well above average in intelligence. Grant has proved himself to be a very good NCO with a well developed sense of duty and loyalty to his Regiment. He is sober minded conscientious and thoroughly trustworthy, and has considerable personal initiative.

I have no hesitation in recommending him to any employer.

The above assessments
have been read to me.
Signature of Soldier..... *Hugh T Grant*.....

Place..... *ALDERSHOT*..... *(Signature of C.O.)*

Date..... *10 June 60*..... *1st Bn The Para Regt*..... Unit

CHAPTER 16

Where are they now?

December 2000

> From quiet beginnings
> Out to the undiscovered end,
> There's nothing worth the wear of living,
> But laughter – and the love of friends!

THE AUTHOR – HUGH GRANT – With his return to his home town of Inverness in June 1960 he embarked on a lengthy and fairly undistinguished career in the hotel industry. His tendency to being accident prone still continued to dog him but it allowed him and his wife Joan to raise their five children. After some 25 years in hotel management he found himself for reasons that would take too long to explain looking for a fresh career. There followed a character forming period during which he dabbled in estate agency and insurance, acted as an agent for a French wine company, peddled water filters and managed a public bar complex.

In 1990 in partnership with his wife Joan they set up their family business of Heraldic Art and Design with outlets in Inverness, Loch Ness, Edinburgh and York. The business continues to expand giving him freedom to develop his other interest of free lance writing. The setting up of his own book publishing business will be the vehicle for this in the future. Apart from trying to organise his eight grandchildren he seeks refuge in Loch Ness Rotary Club and is Founder Chairman of the Highlands and Islands Branch of the Parachute Regimental Association.

ARTHUR 'WOLF' LILES – After demob in 1960 Arthur married Brenda and settled in Colchester in Essex. In 1967 they emigrated to Australia, along with their two daughters, and settled in Sydney in New South Wales. Arthur is employed as Sales Manager for an engineering company that distributes mechanical transmission products for the State of New South Wales. Arthur and Brenda have three grandchildren.

HENRY ARMSTRONG – After demob from 2 Para Henry returned to his native North-east and worked in a limestone quarry for a Scottish Company as a dump truck driver. Then followed a twenty year stretch driving for Vaux Breweries in Sunderland. For the next nine years he was steward of a workingmens social club in Houghton-le-Spring before ill health brought about early retirement.

Henry lives in retirement with his wife Margaret in Hetton-le-Hole.

JOHN 'WOODY' WOOD – Demobbed along with his great pal Henry Woody too returned to the North-east and worked as a shot firer (explosives) in the same quarry. About this time Woody became Henry's brother-in-law when he married Henry's sister Rose. He later started work in a National Coal Board supply depot in the North Durham area until he was made redundant as the mines gradually closed. This was followed by a triple heart bypass which finally put paid to his working days.

ROLAND 'BLACKIE' GAMBLE – Champion Recruit of 124 Platoon – No information has been traced on his whereabouts.

SERGEANT BRIAN SHARMAN – Platoon Sergeant of 124 Platoon. Not much information except that he became a Regimental Sergeant Major at a later date.

COMPANY SERGEANT MAJOR FRED 'GOG' GRAHAM – Research shows that Major F.W. Graham MBE served as Quartermaster with 15th Para (TA) in Glasgow from April 1980 to January 1983. He was succeeded in this post by Captain George Brown who in an earlier life was Cpl George Brown of 'C' Company, 1 Para.

Last unconfirmed report was that Major F.W. Graham (retd) was running a market garden business somewhere in Wales.

H 'NOBBY' ARNOLD – Nobby one of the really great characters of 1 Para went on to become an RSM in his own right. Now living in retirement near Worthing.

PHIL 'PADDY' TOMKINS – After demob he had a brief spell as an assistant cinema manager before going on to forge a considerable career in the Ice Cream business and now operates a consultancy business to that trade in Manchester.

His interest in the Army and all things military never waned as he served in the TA for many years then as an instructor with the Army Cadet Force.

On November 2000 he was appointed RSM of the Merseyside Cadet Force. He lives with Maree in Tyldesley with four grown up children and five grandchildren.

GEORGE BROWN – Retired in 1988 from the Army with the rank of Major. Champion Recruit of Platoon No 67 as a young soldier he took part in the Suez landings and his final action was in the Falklands War.

Employed since retirement as a regional Facilities Manager with Siemens the international conglomerate he lives near Farnborough with his wife June and three daughters and three grandchildren.

JAMES 'JIM' HUNT – After his demob in 1960 Jim went back to his trade as an engineer in Southampton. Former Champion recruit of 109 Platoon.

Married to Hazel with one son James who served with the Marines for some 12 years as a PTI (Physical Training Instructor). Jim's father also served in the Marines. This break in the family Marine tradition is explained by Jim as follows. When called up for N.S. he found that the day he attended for some reason they were not taking Marine applicants that particular day and as Jim could not afford the bus fare or taking time off work to come back another day he found himself joining the Paras.

DAVID 'MITCH' MITCHELL – Great personal friend of Jim Hunt as they had come through depot together into 'C' Company, 1 Para and were known as the Terrible Twins. Mitch left the Army in 1961 and after a variety of jobs started up his own free lance Photographic business in the early 1970's.

At the time of the Lockerbie air disaster he was one of the first media people on the scene and took the famous photograph of the crashed aircraft's fuselage lying in the field outside the town. Married with two sons and two daughters he lives in Balloch near Loch Lomond.

BRIAN 'PLODDY' HODGSON – Brian retired early in 2000 after a long career with the Atomic Energy Commission. Past Chairman of the West Cumbria branch of the Parachute Regimental Association and Treasurer for some 35 years. Married to Joan with four daughters and seven grandchildren and resides in Workington.

DENNIS PURTON – Married to Muriel and operates his own international flooring business in Stoke-on-Trent. Dennis and Muriel have seven children and no less than seventeen grandchildren!

JAMES 'JIM' WILKIE – Returned to Aberdeen University in 1961 and took his Honours Degree and married Nancy some three days after his Final Exams.

Thereafter he taught in various schools, lectured in Aberdeen University, published two educational books, became a National Development officer and a Scottish Exam, Board Moderator. Since 1987 Jim has been working in Financial Services with the J. Rothschild Partnership. Finally retired in November 2000 and now lives in retirement with Nancy in Dalgety Bay in Fife.

LT R.D. 'RUDGE' PENLEY – Tragically killed in a parachuting accident in 1961.

FRANK BRADY – Frank transferred in 1960 from 1 Para to 9 Independent Para Squadron Royal Engineers. In 1968 he took a purchase discharge from the Army and enlisted as a private soldier in the Australian Army. Served in South Vietnam and wounded in action but returned as an Advisor to the army of the Republic of Vietnam. Commissioned in 1974 and served until 1993 when he had completed his army service with the rank of Major. Continued working as a consultant for the Australian Department of Defence. Now living happily in retirement, enjoying his fishing, in Forster, New South Wales with wife Helen.

"GARY" – The one who almost launched the unsuspecting author into a lucrative career as a pimp! After leaving the Forces "Gary" clearly moved into a different league putting his hard earned 'C' Company education to good effect. This resulted in him going down for a 12 year stretch for armed robbery in the mid 70's. His code name of "Gary" will suffice just in case he is trying to go straight after his release.

JOHN 'JENNY' WREN – Tragically killed in a car crash somewhere in Africa early in the 1960's.

TEX BANWELL – Keith Demer 'Tex' Banwell passed away in 1999 at the age of 81 years after a truly eventful life lived to the full. He is survived by his wife Anne and three children from a previous marriage.

DOREEN WRIGHT – After the air disaster in August 1959 a number of coffins were brought back to this country for a symbolic funeral ceremony. The burial took place and the memorial that names 27 of the victims stands in Brookwood Cemetery in Surrey. In the late summer of 2000 contact was made with Doreen's family through their local paper the "South Shields Gazette".

The author travelled south to meet up with Doreen's widowed mother 87 year old Mrs Abigail Wright and her aunt Mrs Ellen Steel. He presented them with the photograph that he had taken of Doreen on the Notre Dame bridge some forty years earlier.

THE MOUSETRAP – The World's longest running play and now in its 49th Year! The Agatha Christie play opened on 25th November 1952 and is still running . . . On December 16th 2000 it celebrated its 20,000th performance and a celebratory lunch was held in the Savoy to mark this landmark in the history of the British theatre. Present was the luckiest man in showbiz: Matthew Pritchard, Agatha Christie's grandson. His grandmother gave him the stage rights on his ninth birthday. The London production alone is said to have netted him £30 million alone.

Not present will be the two unluckiest men in showbiz: The producers who bought the film rights to The Mousetrap in 1956 for £10,000, on condition that they could not start filming until the West End production closed.

Both men died waiting.

In 1975, on a business trip to London, the author felt duty bound to see the play.